Angola:

Malaria Operational Plan FY 2014

Table of Contents

ABBREVIATIONS

ACTs	artemisinin-based combination therapy
AL	artemether-lumefantrine
ANC	antenatal clinic
AS/AQ	artesunate-amodiaquine
BCC	behavior change communication
CDC	Centers for Disease Control and Prevention
CECOMA	Central Unit for Procurement and Provision of Medicines and Medical Supplies (*Central de Compras de Medicamentos de Angola*)
DHP	dihydroartemisinin-piperaquine
DNME	National Directorate of Medicines and Equipment (*Direcção Nacional de Medicamentos e Equipamentos*)
DPS	Provincial Health Directorate (*Direcção Provincial da Saúde*)
EPI	expanded program on immunization
EPR	epidemic preparedness and response
FBO	faith-based organization
FELTP	Field Epidemiology and Laboratory Training Program
Global Fund	Global Fund to Fight AIDS, Tuberculosis, and Malaria
GHI	Global Health Initiative
GRA	Government of Angola
HMIS	health information management system
IMCI	integrated management of childhood illness
IPTp	intermittent preventive treatment for pregnant women
IRS	indoor residual spraying
ITN	insecticide treated net
LLIN	long-lasting insecticide treated net
M&E	monitoring and evaluation
MIS	Malaria Indicator Survey
MOH	Ministry of Health
MOP	Malaria Operational Plan
NGOs	nongovernmental organizations
NMCP	National Malaria Control Program
PMI	President's Malaria Initiative
RDT	rapid diagnostic test
SP	sulfadoxine-pyrimethamine
UNICEF	United Nations Children's Fund
USAID	United States Agency for International Development
WHO	World Health Organization

I. EXECUTIVE SUMMARY

Malaria prevention and control are major foreign assistance objectives of the U.S. Government. In May 2009, President Barack Obama announced the Global Health Initiative (GHI), a six-year, comprehensive effort to reduce the burden of disease and promote healthy communities and families around the world. Through the GHI, the United States will help partner countries improve health outcomes, with a particular focus on improving the health of women, newborns, and children.

The President's Malaria Initiative (PMI) is a core component of the GHI, along with HIV/AIDS and tuberculosis. PMI was launched in June 2005 as a five-year, $1.2 billion initiative to rapidly scale up malaria prevention and treatment interventions and reduce malaria-related mortality by 50% in 15 high-burden countries in sub-Saharan Africa. With passage of the 2008 Lantos-Hyde Act, funding for PMI was extended and, as part of GHI, the goal of PMI was adjusted to reduce malaria-related mortality by 70% in the original 15 countries by the end of 2015. Programming of PMI activities follows the core principles of GHI: encouraging country ownership and investing in country-led plans and health systems; increasing impact and efficiency through strategic coordination and programmatic integration; strengthening and leveraging key partnerships, multilateral organizations, and private contributions; implementing a woman- and girl-centered approach; improving monitoring and evaluation; and promoting research and innovation.

Angola was selected as one of the first three countries in PMI in June 2005. Given the almost three-decade-long civil war, which ended in 2002, implementation of large-scale malaria control activities in Angola has faced serious challenges. The country's health infrastructure was severely damaged during the war, and it is estimated that only about 40% of the population has access to government health facilities. Significant progress has been made in malaria control, with the decrease in malaria parasitemia falling from 21.1% in the 2006/7 Malaria Indicator Survey (MIS) to 13.5% in the 2011 MIS, a reduction of almost 40%. However, malaria continues to be a major health problem, accounting for an estimated 35% of the overall mortality in children under five years of age, 25% of maternal mortality, and 60% of hospital admissions for children under five years of age. Malaria transmission is highest in northern Angola, while the southern provinces have highly seasonal malaria.

In February 2009, Angola signed a five-year, $78-million Round 7 malaria grant from the Global Fund to Fight AIDS, Tuberculosis and Malaria (Global Fund). Angola was also successful in a Global Fund Round 10 grant for malaria for $111 million. The grants were consolidated and after some delays, were signed on June 15, 2012. The United Nations Children's Fund and the World Health Organization have been major partners of the National Malaria Control Program (NMCP) in scaling up interventions. An effective partnership with ExxonMobil has resulted in donations of $4.5 million to the United States Agency for International Development (USAID) over the last seven years to further PMI and Government of the Republic of Angola's (GRA) efforts in the fight against malaria.

PMI has begun discussions with the NMCP on possible transition strategies and different programmatic scenarios to adapt to Angola's growing prosperity. These discussions are timely, since the GRA is increasing its commitment to health through yearly increases in funding and is focusing specifically on reducing maternal and child morbidity and mortality, as well as strengthening cross-border malaria control and elimination efforts.

This PMI Malaria Operational Plan for fiscal year (FY) 2014 for Angola was developed during a planning visit carried out in April 2013 by representatives from USAID, the Centers for Disease Control and Prevention, and the Angolan NMCP, with participation of other major partners working on malaria in country. PMI's proposed FY 2014 activities are based on experiences and progress during the last seven years, the NMCP's 2011-2015 National Malaria Control Strategy, and the strategic planning process that the USAID/Angola mission is currently developing. PMI activities are designed to complement activities supported by other partners.

With the proposed FY 2014 PMI funding of $27,000,000, the following activities will be supported:

Insecticide treated nets: The NMCP recently launched the first national universal coverage campaign of long-lasting insecticide treated nets. Universal coverage, in Angola, is defined as one insecticide-treated net for every two residents. PMI has been supporting this campaign through net procurement (nearly 1.7 million to date) and distribution, as well as assisting the NMCP at the national level in planning and coordination of the campaign. The estimated need to reach universal coverage is over 11 million nets, with 7.8 million available or promised. The GRA plans to cover the gap with the help of donors. This campaign is expected to be completed by early/mid 2014. Prior to this campaign, PMI supported multiple channels of net distribution: mass campaigns, routine distribution through antenatal care clinics, expanded program on immunization clinics and Municipal Health Days, and sale of subsidized nets.

With FY 2014 funds, PMI plans to continue to support the routine "keep-up" strategy of distribution to pregnant women and children under five years of age to ensure new families and children are covered. With many residents unable to afford the cost of a net, PMI will continue to support the existing MOH strategy of providing nets free of charge. With FY 2014 funding, it is expected that about 1.45 million long-lasting insecticide-treated nets will be procured and distributed free to pregnant women and children under five years of age through routine clinic services (antenatal care and immunization) together with behavior change communication activities to increase demand for and correct use of nets.

Indoor residual spraying (IRS): PMI has supported IRS in selected provinces since 2006. In the last 12 months, PMI sprayed 145,264 structures, protecting a total population of more than 689,668 residents in the provinces of Huila, Huambo, and Cunene. More than 96% of the houses targeted for spraying were sprayed. In FY 2013, PMI will stop IRS activities in Cunene and Huila Provinces, but continue to support IRS in Huambo Province, in Bailundo and two other municipalities, in order to concentrate PMI's IRS efforts and work with the GRA to assume financial and operational responsibility for the program. These same municipalities are to be covered in FY 2014. PMI plans to support epidemiological and entomological monitoring in both the provinces where IRS has stopped and in Huambo and to continue routine environmental monitoring to ensure all IRS activities comply with environmental regulations and requirements.

Malaria in pregnancy: According to the 2011 Integrated Survey of Population Welfare, 69% of women in Angola attend an antenatal care clinic at least once during their pregnancy (and 47% attend all four recommended visits). Nonetheless, IPTp (at least two doses of the recommended drug) rates remain low at 18%, according to the 2011 MIS, mostly due to a weak health system. PMI has supported Angola's NMCP scale-up of IPTp through health worker training and behavior change communication activities to promote early and regular attendance at antenatal care clinics. Together with other partners, IPTp is now being implemented in all 161 municipalities nationwide.

With FY 2014 funding, efforts to promote early antenatal clinic attendance, increase the number of pregnant women receiving at least two doses of IPTp, and distribute free insecticide-treated nets to pregnant women through antenatal clinics are planned to continue. PMI plans to continue its support for health worker training and supervision and support the NMCP to ensure a steady supply of commodities for the prevention and treatment of malaria in pregnancy.

Case management: For the past five years, PMI has been supporting improved parasitological diagnosis of malaria with rapid diagnostic tests (RDTs) and microscopy through procurement of equipment and supplies and training and supervision of laboratory workers. In collaboration with other partners and support from PMI, treatment with an artemisinin-based combination therapy (ACT), namely artemether-lumefantrine, has now been implemented in all health facilities nationwide. In FY 2013, PMI procured approximately 3.8 million artemether-lumefantrine treatments and 900,000 RDTs.

With the expectation that malaria prevalence will continue to decline, with FY 2014 funding, PMI plans to temporarily increase support for RDT procurement to ensure that all suspected cases of malaria are parasitologically diagnosed, while working with the GRA and other partners to procure greater numbers of ACTs and RDTs approved by a recognized quality control body. PMI plans to procure approximately 1,300,000 multispecies RDTs and supplies for microscopy, as well as continue to support the training and supervision of laboratory workers in laboratory diagnosis of malaria. PMI plans also to procure approximately an additional 700,000 artemether-lumefantrine treatments to help cover the ACT gap left after GRA makes its procurement.

Through local and international nongovernmental organization, PMI plans to continue to support strengthening of malaria diagnosis and treatment at the health facility level as well as to support strengthening of planning and supervision at municipality and provincial levels. .PMI also plans to support the NMCP to conduct joint supervision and to provide on-the-job training to health personnel in the provinces. With completion of the successful PMI-supported pilot study of private sector sales of ACTs in Huambo Province, PMI plans to continue to support the expansion of private sector sales of subsidized ACTs to Uige Province.

In addition, PMI plans to continue to provide technical assistance to promote good supply chain management and commodities security through the central medical stores. Together with the European Union, and other partners, PMI plans to continue to provide technical assistance in pharmaceutical management to the NMCP and National Essential Drugs Program at the central, provincial, and district levels.

Behavior Change Communication: Community mobilization, sensitization, and behavior change efforts have increased in recent years, especially with the commencement of the universal coverage ITN campaign. Nonetheless, the 2011 MIS showed that nearly 30% of women interviewed did not know that mosquitoes cause malaria and the same percentage did not know that using mosquito nets can prevent malaria.

With FY 2014 funds, PMI will support mass media messaging on all aspects of malaria prevention and control, as well as support increased interpersonal communication to reinforce healthy behavior change.

Monitoring and evaluation: The NMCP has consistently highlighted a lack of quality and timely data as a key challenge in the malaria program. PMI supported both the 2006/7 and 2011 MIS, which provided key data on parasitemia and coverage of malaria control and prevention interventions. With FY 2013 funds PMI will support, with the help of the Global Fund, the next MIS, expected to take place in 2014. PMI has also supported health management information system strengthening, monitoring of the therapeutic efficacy of first-line antimalarials, and surveys to assess availability of malaria commodities at health facilities.

With FY 2014 funds, PMI plans to continue to support strengthening of the health management information system based on a new draft MOH strategy. PMI also plans to support biannual surveys of health facilities and provincial medical stores to monitor the availability of key malaria commodities, including those procured by PMI, and to conduct enhanced surveillance in IRS districts to help guide more effective application of future IRS activities. In addition, a second round of therapeutic efficacy studies of antimalarials is to be supported.

Health systems strengthening and integration: In line with GHI principles, PMI has reinforced its efforts to build capacity and integrate activities across programs. Because of the limited access of the population to government health facilities in the rural areas of most provinces, PMI has supported nongovernmental organizations and faith-based organizations that have a presence at the provincial level and work closely with provincial health authorities. These nongovernmental organizations assist with training and supervision of health workers on malaria as part of Integrated Management of Childhood Illnesses, supply chain management at the provincial level and below, and behavior change communication activities to ensure correct usage of long-lasting insecticide-treated nets, IPTp, RDTs, and ACTs. National or international nongovernmental are currently being supported in 9 of the country's 18 provinces through a combination of PMI funding and an annual donation to USAID/Angola from the ExxonMobil Foundation. These organizations also provide support for municipal health budget planning and strengthening of HIV service delivery through an integrated USAID program. PMI also supports the Centers for Disease Control and Prevention Field Epidemiology and Laboratory Training Program, which trains Angolan nationals through didactic and practical training opportunities in public health and malaria. In addition, the supply chain system strengthening support is integrated for multiple diseases.

With FY 2014 funding, PMI plans to continue to support these integrated programs to deliver quality service to patients and to ensure that adequate commodities are available to diagnose and treat patients with suspected and confirmed malaria.

II. STRATEGY

INTRODUCTION

In May 2009, President Barack Obama announced the Global Health Initiative (GHI), a comprehensive effort to reduce the burden of disease and promote healthy communities and families around the world. Through the GHI, the U.S. Government (USG) will invest to help partner countries improve health outcomes, with a particular focus on improving the health of women, newborns, and children. The GHI is a global commitment to invest in healthy and productive lives, building upon and expanding the USG's successes in addressing specific diseases and issues.

The President's Malaria Initiative (PMI) is a core component of a comprehensive effort to reduce the burden of disease and promote healthy communities and families worldwide. PMI was launched in June 2005 as a 5-year, $1.2 billion initiative to rapidly scale up malaria prevention and treatment interventions and reduce malaria-related mortality by 50% in 15 high-burden countries in sub-Saharan Africa. With passage of the 2008 Lantos-Hyde Act, funding for PMI was extended, and as part of the GHI, the goal of PMI was adjusted to reduce malaria-related mortality by 70% in the original 15 countries by the end of 2015. This will be achieved by continuing to scale up coverage of the most vulnerable groups—children under five years of age and pregnant women—with proven preventive and therapeutic interventions, including artemisinin-based combination treatments (ACTs), insecticide-treated bed nets (ITNs), intermittent preventive treatment for pregnant women (IPTp), and indoor residual spraying (IRS).

Angola was one of the first three countries selected as a PMI target country in 2005, and PMI has supported activities in the country since that time. Large-scale implementation of ACTs and IPTp began in 2006 and has progressed rapidly with support from PMI and other partners. ACTs and IPTp are now available and being used in all public health facilities nationwide and PMI has supported the distribution of more than six million long-lasting insecticide treated bed nets (LLINs) to pregnant women and children under five in the last seven years. In Angola, PMI works with the Ministry of Health (MOH) through the National Malaria Control Program (NMCP) and coordinates with other national and international partners, including the Global Fund Against AIDS, Tuberculosis, and Malaria (Global Fund), United Nations organizations, numerous nongovernmental organizations, faith-based organizations, and the private sector.

This Malaria Operational Plan (MOP) presents a detailed implementation plan to be implemented primarily in calendar year 2015. It is based on the PMI Multi-Year Strategy and Plan and the NMCP's current 5-Year Strategy (2011-2015). This MOP was developed in consultation with the NMCP and with participation of national and international partners involved with malaria prevention and control in the country. PMI proposes activities that support and complement the National Malaria Control Strategy and Plan and that build on investments made by PMI and other partners, including the Global Fund, to improve and expand malaria-related services. This document briefly reviews the current status of malaria control policies and interventions in Angola, describes progress to date, identifies challenges and unmet needs if the targets of the NMCP and PMI are to be achieved, and provides a description of planned FY 2014 activities. PMI has begun discussions with the NMCP on a phased transition from support for commodity procurement and IRS, given the increase in the Government of the Republic of Angola (GRA) budget for health.

MALARIA SITUATION IN ANGOLA

The National Institute of Statistics of Angola estimates the population in 2015 will be 22,675,168. All are at risk for malaria, but there is significant heterogeneity in transmission, with hyperendemicity in northeastern Angola, including Cabinda Province, an enclave in the north of the country. The central and coastal areas are largely mesoendemic with stable transmission. The four southern provinces bordering Namibia have highly seasonal transmission and are prone to epidemics. In the north, the peak malaria transmission season extends from March to May, with a secondary peak in October-November.

Significant progress has been made in the fight against malaria in Angola, and data from the 2011 Malaria Indicator Survey (MIS) show an almost 50% decline in parasitemia among children under five years of age from the 2006/7 MIS (from 21% to 13.5%). The largest declines in parasitemia among children were in the south; unstable transmission zones, where the change represents a nearly 60% drop (from 21% to 9%); and in the capital, where a 70% decline (from 6% to 1.8%) was observed when data from MIS 2006/7 and MIS 2011 were compared. According to the 2011 MIS, the mortality rate for children under five has fallen by 23% over the last five years, and it is currently estimated at 91 deaths per 1,000 live births.

In 2012, there were 3,026,125 reported cases (confirmed and suspected) of malaria reported in the public sector in Angola, with 5,736 deaths (NMCP 2013). The majority of cases of malaria are caused by *Plasmodium falciparum* (87%); *P. vivax, P. malariae*, and *P. ovale* represented 7%, 3%, and 3% of cases, respectively (NMCP 2012 data). The primary vectors in high transmission areas are *Anopheles gambiae s.s.* and *An. funestus*, which are endophilic and endophagic; in coastal areas, *An. melas* may be an important vector, and *An. pharaoensis* can be a secondary vector where present (Fortes, NMCP 2013).

While the southern part of the country is considered epidemic-prone, and the southern province of Cuando Cubango did experience an outbreak in early 2013, the northern, hyperendemic areas (Lunda Norte, Uige, Zaire Provinces) of the country also experienced upsurges in malaria reports in 2012 and early 2013. A PMI-supported study carried out in 2008 showed that malaria transmission in the city of Luanda was very low, except in the outlying municipalities of Cacuaco, Viana, and Samba.[1] However, these same municipalities) also experienced an increase in reported malaria cases in 2012 and early 2013.

---

[1] Thwing J Mihigo J , Pataca Fernandes A, Saute F, Ferreira C, Fortes F, Macedo de Oliveira A, Newman RD 2009. How Much Malaria Occurs in Urban Luanda, Angola? A Health Facility-Based Assessment. *Am. J. Trop. Med. Hyg.,* 80(3), pp. 487–491

Figure 1: Malaria Transmission in Angola

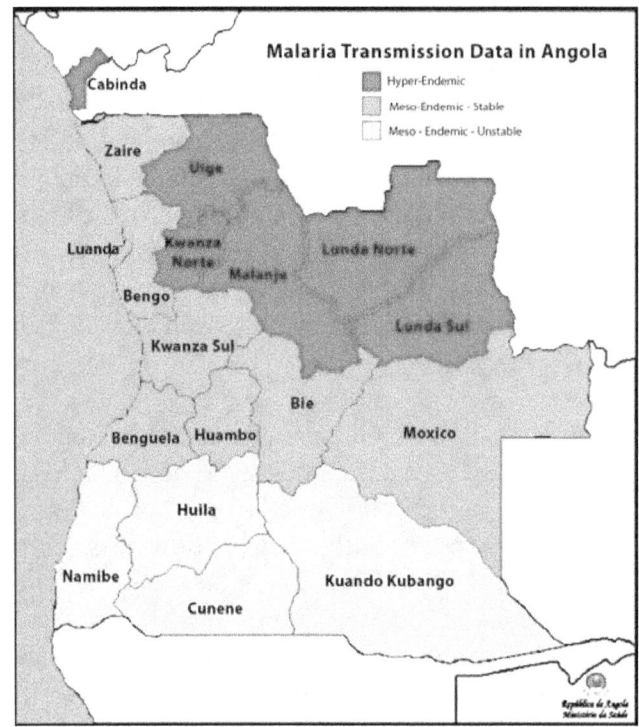

HEALTH SERVICE DELIVERY SYSTEM AND ORGANIZATION OF THE MINISTRY OF HEALTH

Approximately 40% of the Angolan population uses the public sector for healthcare in Angola, and there is notable disparity between urban and rural inhabitants.[2] Similar to other countries in Africa, the Angolan National Health System has three levels of care: primary care, in which basic care is provided through health posts, health centers, and municipal hospitals; secondary care, in which care is provided through general (provincial) hospitals; and tertiary care, in which specialized care is provided through central hospitals in the capital city of Luanda.

Because the country is still recovering from nearly three decades of war, the GRA has focused a significant number of resources on rebuilding infrastructure, including health infrastructure, which was severely damaged during the conflict, with the number of health facilities increasing from 952 in 2003 to 2,376 in 2011.[3] In addition, the GRA has prioritized increasing human resources for health (the number of doctors tripled from 2005 to 2009[4]), but there is still a critical shortage and inequitable distribution of health workers; for example, in 2009 there were an estimated 18 doctors per 100,000 population and 85% of health workers work in urban areas.[5]

[2] Connor, Catherine, Denise Averbug, and Maria Miralles. 2010. *Angola Health System Assessment 2010.* Bethesda, MD: Health Systems 20/20, Abt Associates Inc.
[3] Angola Health System Assessment 2010.
[4] Angola Health System Assessment 2010.
[5] Angola Health System Assessment 2010; data for the estimation of number of doctors per 100,000 population uses number of doctors cited from the Angola Health System Assessment and the estimated population cited in the FY 2009 MOP.

Since the late 1990s, the GRA has embarked upon various degrees of administrative and more recently, fiscal, decentralization. A new law grants municipal governments authorities for budgeting, managing, and implementing their own pool of funds. In an attempt to drastically improve public services, the GRA in 2012 transferred over $400 million dollars to municipal governments, mostly to carry out health services. Next to be decentralized are water and education services, where funds will be allocated directly to the municipalities. Over the next three years, over $2 billion will be allocated to these sub-national units through various policy directives already in place.

The MOH has four levels of administration: the national, provincial, municipal, and health facility. The central level includes the Directorate of the Ministry (including the NMCP), where national guidelines and norms are elaborated, adapted, or adopted, and the national technical direction is set. The provincial level, which includes the Provincial Health Directorate (DPS), is responsible for coordinating all health activities in the province and providing oversight to the general (provincial) hospitals. The municipal level provides technical and operational directives to municipal hospitals, local health centers, and posts. The administration of each health facility provides direct supervision for the day-to-day operation of the health unit and health staff, but each facility depends on the municipality for budget and procurement. In 2008, the MOH initiated a process of revitalization of municipal health services to improve provision of the essential package of health services. The vision is to decentralize administration and to increasingly empower municipal administrative levels with the responsibility and the resources to ensure access to quality health services. As of 2011, municipalities now receive their own funding ($2 million) for health and can plan health activities independently of the provincial level.

The NMCP has 60 staff members, 52 of which are currently supported through grants from the Global Fund. The NMCP is headed by a director, who is supported by a central team responsible for epidemiology, entomology, case management, monitoring and evaluation (M&E), behavior change communication (BCC), finance, and administration, as well as a provincial team. The NMCP collaborates with related programs of the National Directorate of Public Health, namely Reproductive Health, Integrated Management of Childhood Illnesses (IMCI), Epidemiology, as well as the National Essential Drugs Program, National Institute for the Fight against HIV/AIDS, the National Institute of Public Health, and other services and directorates of the MOH as necessary. The NMCP has tried to strengthen its health infrastructure by retraining staff and placing provincial malaria officers in all 18 provinces. Every province now has a provincial malaria focal person paid by the Ministry, and a provincial malaria officer, supported by the Global Fund. Together they coordinate all malaria activities, engage in joint supervision of commodities and case management practices with the DPS staff, and provide training to all health providers in the province. At the municipal level, municipal malaria focal persons are responsible for M&E of malaria program activities, and work in collaboration with provincial malaria officers. Provincial malaria officers at provincial level are embedded within the DPS and are under the direct supervision of the provincial health director, whereas the officers at the central level supported by the Global Fund work directly with the NMCP central-level team within the National Institute of Public Health and report to the NMCP director.

MALARIA CONTROL STRATEGY FOR ANGOLA

The GRA has made firm commitments to reduce mortality and morbidity due to malaria in the country. To achieve its goals, the NMCP has adopted the following operational strategies, as stated in the current Malaria Control Strategic Plan (2011-2015):

- Decentralization of malaria control interventions in accordance with current efforts to decentralize health and other government services to municipal levels;
- Early diagnosis of all suspected malaria cases using microscopy or rapid diagnostic test (RDT);
- Prompt and effective treatment of uncomplicated malaria cases with ACTs and timely treatment of severe cases;
- Increased uptake of IPTp with sulfadoxine-pyrimethamine (SP) through improved antenatal care (ANC) services;
- Integrated vector management comprising bed net distribution, IRS, and larviciding;
- Enhanced surveillance and rapid epidemic detection in southern provinces at risk of epidemics;
- Improved BCC on malaria prevention at the community level;
- Strengthened partnerships and supporting cross-border initiatives.

Malaria diagnosis: In the past, malaria was diagnosed in most facilities based on clinical signs and symptoms. Malaria microscopy was only available in hospitals and larger health centers and the quality of diagnosis varied considerably between sites. RDTs were introduced in Angola in 2006 and used whenever available. In accordance with the change in WHO guidance related to malaria laboratory diagnosis in 2010, Angola updated its strategic plan (2011-2015) to align with international standards, which recommends that all suspected cases of malaria be diagnosed parasitologically, using either microscopy or RDTs. The policy has been widely disseminated in the form of NMCP communications and trainings, but problems still exist in terms of scaling up high-quality parasitologic diagnosis of malaria. These include shortages of RDTs, a limited laboratory network, inadequate quality control procedures, and perhaps the greatest challenge— failure of health workers to appropriately follow the results of laboratory and RDT testing when prescribing treatment.

Malaria treatment: Artemether-lumefantrine (AL) is first-line therapy for malaria, but since May 2006, AL and artesunate-amodiaquine (AS/AQ) have been used as alternative first-line drugs for the treatment of uncomplicated malaria. The NMCP decided to introduce AS/AQ as an alternative first-line drug because fixed-dose combination AS/AQ therapy includes fewer tablets than AL in an adult treatment, thereby facilitating improved adherence. In addition, AL was not recommended for children under five kilograms; as of 2010, the NMCP procures the co-formulated AS/AQ, Co-Arsucam®. The NMCP also engaged in a large multicenter drug efficacy study of a fix-dosed formulation of dihydroartemisinin-piperaquine (DHP) and now includes it as another treatment. The Chinese government has provided continuous donations of DHP. A drug efficacy study was conducted in 2011 to determine if DHP is effective and safe in the Angolan population, but was not finished due to implementation delays. The NMCP and PMI are currently conducting a therapeutic efficacy study of both AL and DHP with results expected in mid to late 2013.

Malaria in Pregnancy: The NMCP's policy on malaria in pregnancy consists of a three-pronged approach made up of use of ITNs, IPTp with at least two doses of SP, and prompt and effective case management of acute malaria. IPTp was adopted as national policy in 2004. This policy currently applies to the entire country, including the epidemic-prone areas in the south. According to reports from the Reproductive Health Department, routine site visits conducted by representatives from the department, provincial malaria supervisors, and provincial malaria officers indicate the policy is being implemented. Supervision is conducted at all health facilities that provide the essential health package, which includes ANC. (Thus, health posts are not supervised as they do not provide ANC services.) Angola is in the process of updating its policy for malaria in pregnancy to incorporate the 2012 World Health Organization (WHO) guidance on IPTp administration. The 2011 MIS found that only 17.5% of women reported taking at least two IPTp doses during their last pregnancy.

Vector management: The NMCP Malaria Strategic Plan 2011-2015 promotes an integrated vector management strategy that includes increased ownership and use of ITNs, IRS in epidemic-prone areas, and larviciding. The country is in the midst of a universal coverage campaign distributing ITNs. In the past, it has distributed nets through mass campaigns, routine distribution channels, and subsidized sales. The NMCP also supports the use of IRS for malaria prevention in epidemic-prone areas and elsewhere in the country. Synthetic pyrethroids are the current insecticides of choice based on susceptibility and cost-effectiveness. The GRA has banned the use of DDT, and there seems to be no intention in lifting the ban in the near future.

As part of the NMCP's program for integrated vector control, it also employs larviciding, which is fully funded by the GRA. In 2001, Angola conducted a trial of antilarval products in three provinces (Luanda, Cabinda and Namibe), using two kinds of biological larvicides. Since 2008, all 164 municipalities of the country have conducted antilarval activities supported by the GRA and carried out with technical assistance from Cuban entomologists. As part of this activity, larval densities are analyzed, larvicides applied, and densities are re-evaluated post-application to determine larviciding efficacy. Since 2009, this program has applied larvicide to over 4 million square kilometers in all 18 provinces, with efficacy ranging from a 96.7% to 99.7% reduction in mosquito larvae in targeted areas. With technical input from multiple partners, the NMCP is currently planning an extensive evaluation of the larviciding program. The goals are to inform the GRA program and to provide WHO additional data on the effectiveness of larviciding in sub-Saharan Africa.

Epidemic detection and response: The National Epidemiological Surveillance System collects weekly reports on clinically diagnosed cases of malaria from the four epidemic-prone provinces in the south——Namibe, Huila, Cunene, and Cuando Cubango. Since not all districts report on a regular basis and there are delays in releasing reports to the NMCP, these weekly data are currently of limited value for the detecting and containing malaria epidemics.

Funding of malaria control activities Funding of malaria control in Angola is provided by the GRA, with major contributions from PMI, the Global Fund, WHO, United Nations Children's Fund (UNICEF), and private partners, such as ExxonMobil and Chevron, which support specific projects. The overall budget for the MOH is approximately $62.5 million; NMCP's annual budget is about $37.5 million. These funds are used for commodity procurement, larviciding, training and capacity building of health personnel, and general operational costs. National hospitals in Luanda, the provincial hospitals, and some municipal and provincial governments receive budgets directly from the GRA, which also contribute to malaria prevention and treatment. In addition, the GRA has made available $2 million per year to each municipal government for health programs. Municipal governments can access these funds through a formal application process to the MOH.

In 2007, Angola was awarded a $78 million Global Fund Round 7 malaria grant. The MOH is the principal recipient, with WHO, UNICEF, and Population Services International as sub-recipients. The grant was signed in February 2009, and Phase 1 of implementation was completed in October 2010. This grant includes approximately $36 million for ITNs, $17 million for ACTs and case management, $19 million for general health systems strengthening, and $6 million for BCC, over five years.

In 2010, Angola successfully submitted a $111 million Round 10 Global Fund proposal. This proposal, which builds on the accomplishments of Phase 1 of the Round 7 grant and other partner contributions (including PMI), includes approximately $42.5 million for ITNs, $17.0 million for ACTs and case management, $21.7 million for diagnosis, $20.7 million for general health systems strengthening, $1.3 million for BCC, and $7.8 million program management, over five years. The total funding for Year 1 is $21.0 million and for Year 2 is $19.4 million. The NMCP and the Global Fund decided to consolidate the Round 7 and Round 10 grants, which were signed in June 2012, and disbursement of funds began in November 2012, with final disbursement for Phase 1 completed in March 2013.

Since 2006, ExxonMobil has contributed $4.5 million to PMI to support the scale up of ACTs, IPTp, and malaria diagnostics, as well as capacity building and health systems strengthening at health facility, municipal, and provincial levels through the PMI supported USAID Angola NGO strengthening project. This project provides sub-grants to five nongovernmental organizations (NGOs) and faith-based organizations (FBOs) working in eight provinces.

INTEGRATION, COLLABORATION, AND COORDINATION

The NMCP is a department within the National Directorate of Public Health and is responsible for planning, organizing, and supervising all malaria control activities in the country. It works in close collaboration with other departments at the directorate, such as Reproductive Health and Maternal and Child Health, on implementation of malaria in pregnancy and IMCI. There is a continued effort to strengthen working relationships within these departments to coordinate efforts and maximize resources.

The key partners involved in malaria control activities in Angola are MOH, PMI, United Nation agencies (WHO/UNICEF), the Global Fund, Japan International Cooperation Agency (JICA), and various NGOs. With the MOH as the principal recipient of the Global Fund grants, a program management unit was created to work with the NMCP to facilitate the coordination of malaria activities.

Communication and coordination among partners involved in malaria prevention and control in Angola continue to improve due to increasingly strong leadership from the NMCP, which is showing greater willingness to ask for and accept technical support. Other contributing factors include a growing sense of partnership among key international and national organizations and groups supporting the NMCP; greater transparency in terms of funding and activities by all partners; and the catalytic effects of the PMI resident advisors in the NMCP offices, together with the move of several Global Fund-supported national malaria program officers to the NMCP offices. The efforts around ensuring the success of the universal coverage LLIN campaign has led to better integration of the NMCP with other departments of the National Directorate of Public Health, other ministries (Planning and Education), and the armed forces. The national strategy is to integrate LLIN distribution, where feasible, with other campaigns such as polio vaccination at the provincial or even municipal level.

While there are still many weaknesses in coordination of malaria control activities at the central level, the NMCP holds a national meeting at least once a year with donors, partners both at national and provincial level, and all provincial malaria coordinators. These meetings provide an environment where NMCP can work together with malaria provincial representatives to find solutions to challenges faced during the implementation of malaria interventions. During these meetings, the NMCP presents its strategic plan and objectives; provincial supervisors present malaria data by province; and NGOs and other implementing partners also present their activities. Donors have the opportunity to present their budget for the year and outline which program area is supported with their funds; and NGOs and implementing partners in the province also share progress and challenges in malaria control at provincial level.

The Malaria Partners' Forum, made up of civil society and other interested partners focused on malaria, was created in 2007 with the objective of assisting the NMCP with the coordination of partners' activities at all levels and minimize duplication of efforts and resources. Its role is to support the NMCP in coordinating all malaria control activities among malaria partners. The forum was originally under the leadership of PSI, the founding president. After two years, PSI's mandate as president ended, activities under the forum lost some momentum and it was inactive for several years. However, an election was held in 2012 to select new executive leadership, comprised of *Ajuda de Desenvolvimento de Povo para Povo* as president, Chevron and a network of journalists as vice presidents, and technical advisory members. There are about 70 members, including the NMCP, PMI, WHO, UNICEF, local and international NGOs and FBOs, bilateral and multilateral organizations, Angolan military forces, and private sector companies. The Malaria Partners' Forum is also present in some provinces, but coordination of malaria activities at provincial level varies from province to province. The forum is again gaining strength, and over time it will hopefully gain greater recognition, enabling advocacy for additional funding to carry out its activities. Currently, PMI provides the bulk of the support to the operation of the forum.

GOAL AND TARGETS OF THE PRESIDENT'S MALARIA INITIATIVE

The goal of PMI is to reduce malaria-associated mortality by 70% compared to pre-Initiative levels in the 15 original PMI countries and to reduce malaria-associated mortality by 50% in new countries added to PMI in FY 2010 and later. By the end of 2015, PMI will assist Angola to achieve the following targets in populations at risk for malaria:

- >90% of households with a pregnant woman and/or children under five will own at least one ITN;
- 85% of children under five will have slept under an ITN the previous night;
- 85% of pregnant women will have slept under an ITN the previous night;
- 85% of houses in geographic areas targeted for IRS will have been sprayed;
- 85% of pregnant women and children under five will have slept under an ITN the previous night or in a house that has been sprayed with IRS in the last 6 months;
- 85% of women who have completed a pregnancy in the last two years will have received two or more doses of IPTp during that pregnancy; and
- 85% of government health facilities have ACTs available for treatment of uncomplicated malaria.

CURRENT STATUS OF MALARIA INDICATORS

When PMI began work in Angola in December 2005, no accurate, up-to-date information on nationwide coverage of key malaria prevention and control measures was available. To provide the NMCP with information on the status of their control efforts and to establish a baseline for PMI in Angola, a nationwide MIS was conducted between November 2006 and April 2007 with PMI and Global Fund support. This was the first nationwide health survey in more than 20 years in Angola.

At the time the first MIS was conducted in 2006, ACT and IPTp implementation had only just begun, so the figures reported for proportion of children under five years of age receiving an ACT and proportion of pregnant women receiving two doses of IPTp can be considered accurate baselines for PMI. In the case of ITNs, where a large-scale campaign in seven provinces had occurred several months prior to the survey, families interviewed were asked specifically when they had received their bed nets and an adjustment was made in the calculations to take campaign nets into account in estimating the baseline ownership of ITNs.

In 2011 PMI contributed to a second nationwide MIS with an expanded sample size to provide up-to-date information on progress in malaria prevention and treatment activities. The following table shows the baseline and follow-up results for the major indicators being used by PMI:

Indicator	2006–2007 MIS	2011 MIS
Households with at least one ITN	28%*	35%
Children under five years old who slept under an ITN the previous night	18%	26%
Pregnant women who slept under an ITN the previous night	22%	26%
Women who received two or more doses of IPTp	3%	18%

during their last pregnancy in the last two years		
Children under five years old with fever in the last two weeks who received treatment with an ACT within 24 hours of onset of fever	2%	12%

*The estimated PMI baseline before the 2006 measles-ITN mass campaign was 11%.

The table below shows parasitemia at baseline in 2006/2007 MIS compared with 2011 MIS, and demonstrates an almost 40% reduction in parasitemia from 21% to 13.5%.

Malaria Transmission Zones	% Parasitemia 2006/2007*	% Parasitemia 2011
Hyperendemic	31%	25%
Mesoendemic stable	26%	15%
Mesoendemic unstable	21%	9%
Luanda(city)	6%	2%
Total (nationally)	21%	14%

*The 2006/7 figures listed here are from the 2011 MIS report and are different than those published in the 2006/7 MIS.

The table below shows that all-cause under-five mortality decreased from 118 deaths per 1,000 live births in 2001-2006 to 91 deaths per 1,000 live births in 2011. This represents a reduction of under-five mortality by 23%.

Mortality rates for three five-year periods preceding the survey (2011 MIS)						
Years prior to survey	Calendar years	Neonatal mortality (%)	Post-neonatal mortality (%)	Infant mortality (%)	Child mortality (%)	Under 5 mortality (per 1,000)
10-14	1996-2001	29	37	65	56	117
5-9	2001-2006	32	34	67	55	118*
0-4	2006-2011	23	26	50	43	91*

PMI SUPPORT STRATEGY

PMI's strategy for Angola supports the NMCP's strategic goals and priorities and complements the efforts of the GRA and other partners. PMI prioritizes the key intervention areas and supports capacity building at all levels of the health system. PMI has focused on supporting comprehensive malaria services in geographic areas with high malaria transmission and a concentrated population. IRS focused on two epidemic-prone provinces in the south and Huambo Province, which, at the start of PMI's IRS program, had the second highest incidence of malaria. These high-burden provinces also contain priority districts under the draft USAID Angola Country Development Cooperation Strategy so that PMI investments are also leveraging other health and development program investments in integrated regional projects prioritized by the mission.

With FY 2014 funding. PMI plans to leverage USG's regional integration strategy to strengthen and improve service delivery through continuing to build capacity of NMCP while:

- Strengthening provincial-, municipal-, and health facility-level technical capacity, as well as strengthening local NGO and FBO capacity;
- Refocusing IRS strategy based on epidemiologic and entomologic data to reflect the current risk of malaria;
- Ensuring correct and consistent use of ITNs and nurturing a net culture after the 2013 universal net campaign;
- Improving quality of malaria diagnosis and treatment;
- Increasing access and demand for parasite-based malaria diagnosis and treatment based on results;
- Improving malaria disease surveillance to provide evidence-based data to inform the malaria control strategy; and
- Focusing on PMI-supported program implementation monitoring to ensure investments are delivering expected results.

The GRA has been progressively increasing its budget for the social sector with a substantial increase in resources for the health sector and for the malaria program. With this potential increase in resources, combined with the possibility of a reduction in funding for malaria from the USG after the expiration of the Lantos-Hyde, PMI and the NMCP are beginning discussions about a transition strategy: evaluating what resources exist for malaria commodities versus the projected needs and the technical capacity and assistance needed to ensure the country continues to progress in controlling malaria.

III. OPERATIONAL PLAN

PREVENTION ACTIVITIES

Insecticide-treated Nets

Background

Routine distribution to pregnant women and children under five years of age of ITNs through ANC and Expanded Program on Immunization (EPI) clinics and municipal health days (such as World Malaria Day), began in 2001. Mass campaigns did not start until 2006, but were still targeted to vulnerable populations; the first campaign was integrated with polio and measles vaccinations, vitamin A supplementation, and deworming campaign and distributed over 800,000 ITNs to households with children under five years in seven provinces (Cabinda, Uige, Malange, Lunda Norte, Zaire, Moxico and Lunda Sul). In 2010, the NMCP modified the ITN strategy to universal coverage, defined as one net for every two people. In 2011, PMI supported the distribution of 630,000 LLINs through mass universal coverage campaigns in select municipalities in eight provinces (Benguela, Huambo, Kwanza Sul, Kwanza Norte, Zaire, Malange, Uige and Huila). A lot quality assurance sampling survey conducted with PMI support two months after distribution showed that 85% of households had at least one LLIN and 56% had at least one LLIN for every two people in the household.[6]

Procurement and distribution have been supported by multiple partners including the GRA, PMI, Global Fund, UNICEF, UNITAID, Japan International Cooperation Agency, Malaria No More, ExxonMobil Foundation, and Population Services International. In addition, there are nets available in the commercial sector for full price, as well as subsidized nets, supported by PMI and other partners.

Since 2006, approximately 10 million nets have been distributed in the country through various partners, including 6 million from PMI. All strategies have been accompanied by strong BCC messaging to build and support a growing net culture in Angola. While net ownership has increased from 11% in 2006 to 35% in 2011, net usage lags behind significantly:
- 26% of all children under five years slept under a net the previous night;
- 61% of all children under five years slept under a net, among households with at least one ITN;
- 33% of all pregnant women slept under an ITN the night prior to the survey;
- 68% of pregnant women in households with an ITN slept under a net.

The relatively high usage rate among households that have nets signifies that a net culture is growing and that lack of access to nets is a large contributor to the low usage rates in the total population.

---

[6] Rivas, Jorge, Caveya, Elsa. 2011. *ANGOLA (2011): Measuring the scope of the first Universal Coverage campaign of Long-lasting insecticide-treated nets (LLINs) in Benguela, Huambo, Huila, Kwanza Norte, Kwanza Sul, Malanje and Zaire.* Arlington, Va.: USAID/DELIVER PROJECT, Task Order 3.

In early 2013, the GRA and partners launched a nationwide universal distribution campaign to provide one ITN to every two people. An estimated 11.2 million ITNs are needed (approximately 7.8 million nets have already been procured by the GRA, PMI, Global Fund and Japan International Cooperation Agency, through UNICEF. The gap of 3.4 million nets is expected to be filled by the GRA and partners, with the goal of completing the campaign by the end of 2014. Distribution is being done in a phased approach across the country and is accompanied by a strong communications campaign.

Progress during the last 12 months

Since June 2012, PMI's implementing partner, with its substantial experience with community and household distribution in Angola, has provided support to NMCP, conducting training of national and provincial MOH staff on the distribution process. PMI supported the procurement and distribution of 423,000 nets in Kwanza Norte and Zaire Provinces in January 2013 and, later this year, will also support distribution of 1.1 million GRA-purchased nets in two additional provinces (Malange and Uige). In FY 2013, an additional 900,000 PMI-procured ITNs will be distributed in Huambo Province, and by the end of the campaign, PMI will have contributed to universal net ownership in 5 of the 18 provinces in Angola.

The second year of data collection for the ITN durability study was conducted early in 2013 in two municipalities in Uige Province and one in Kwanza Sul Province. Household surveys on net care and use, rapid hole assessments in the field, and hole counting and measurement on-site were conducted. Net samples were collected for WHO cone bioassays and chemical analysis for residual insecticide content at CDC headquarters in Atlanta. While data collection for this study was intended to be conducted annually for three years, it was felt that, given the ongoing universal coverage campaign, there would be little likelihood of finding nets from the original study distribution in year three. Therefore, data collection stopped after year two. Results are expected at the end of 2013. This study will help inform Angola of the timing of future keep-up distribution of nets.

The following table shows a gap analysis developed for the universal coverage campaign in May 2012; adjustments have been made based on GRA's revised procurement plans. PMI will continue to monitor the coverage and procurements and adjust procurement as necessary.

Gap Analysis for ITNs

	2012	2013	2014	2015
Total Population	20,609,294	21,267,300	21,955,773	22,675,168
Total Universal Coverage Needs*	11,449,608	11,815,167	12,197,652	12,597,316
EXPECTED PROCUREMENT FOR CAMPAIGN	*Available*	*Available*	*Available*	*Available*
Angolan Government	1,150,000	1,600,000	3,000,000	not yet known
Global Fund Consolidation Round (R7 Ph2 + R10 Ph1)	2,973,312	212,500		
PMI	900,000	900,000	600,000	
UNICEF		455,000	100,000	100,000
Subtotal LLINs planned for the year	5,023,312	3,167,500	3,700,000	100,000
Subtotal remaining available from previous years (est. nets valid for 3 years)	3,646,601	6,214,942	7,793,119	8,449,656
TOTAL LLINS ALL DONORS	**8,669,913**	**9,382,442**	**11,493,119**	**8,549,656**
GAP TO ACHIEVE UNIVERSAL COVERAGE	**2,779,695**	**2,432,725**	**704,533**	**4,047,660**

	2012	2013	2014	2015
EXPECTED PROCUREMENT FOR ROUTINE DISTRIBUTION	*Available*	*Available*	*Available*	*Available*
Angolan Army	250,000	250,000	250,000	250,000
Angolan Police	50,000	50,000	50,000	50,000
PMI				1,450,000
TOTAL LLINS ALL DONORS	**300,000**	**300,000**	**300,000**	**1,750,000**
GAP TO MAINTAIN UNIVERSAL COVERAGE	**2,479,695**	**2,132,725**	**404,533**	**2,297,660**

*based on one net per 1.8 people.

Proposed activities with FY 2014 funding: ($9,860,000)

The NMCP has not yet clearly defined its "keep-up" strategy after achieving universal coverage in 2014. Historically, the NMCP has not been involved in routine distribution with their own nets, but provinces and municipalities have bought nets with their own funds and distributed them through ANC and EPI clinics and municipal health days. These efforts have been hard to quantify. PMI has discussed with the NMCP conducting the NetCalc workshop to analyze potential keep-up methodologies, but the NMCP requested this happen after the campaign. However, the draft National Malaria Control Strategy 2011-2015 includes language on ensuring pregnant women and children under five years of age have and use nets and expanding the subsidized and full-cost commercial sector for nets. Thus, the keep-up strategy will likely include routine distribution through health facilities, i.e., ANC and EPI clinics, as in the past. The overall annual need for these target populations (pregnant women and children under five years of age) is approximately 4.6 million nets. This will not be sufficient to maintain universal coverage, but will help prevent a precipitous drop.

PMI plans to contribute to maintaining universal coverage with provision of ITNs through routine channels (ANC and EPI clinics) in the eight provinces where PMI supports NGOs. Based on population growth, fertility rate, and access to public health facilities for these target populations, the estimated ITN need will be 1.45 million ITNs. While it is expected that net use will significantly increase after the campaign, Angola does not yet have a net culture, thus support for behavior change is crucial. PMI will continue to focus on proper and consistent use of nets through campaigns that promote behavior change.

1. Procure 1.45 million ITNs for distribution through routine channels including ANC and EPI clinics in eight provinces with PMI-supported NGOs (Zaire, Uige, Malange, Kwanza Norte, Kwanza Sul, Benguela, Huila and Huambo); this quantity is expected to cover the needs of pregnant women and children under five years of age attending ANC and EPI clinics respectively in the public sector. This includes distribution cost to provincial warehouses ($7,975,000).

2. Transfer ITNs from the provincial warehouses to the health facilities in the eight provinces with PMI-supported NGOs. This includes orientation of health staff and M&E costs ($1,885,000).

3. BCC activities at national and local levels to strengthen usage of nets distributed through the universal coverage campaign and through routine channels. Local-level activities will focus primarily on interpersonal communication (costs covered under the BCC section).

Indoor Residual Spraying

Background

In Angola, indoor residual spraying predates PMI, having been initiated by the GRA in Benguela and Cabinda Provinces in 2004. PMI has been supporting large-scale IRS campaigns since 2005, when resources were also leveraged from the Global Fund and WHO to spray selected municipalities in Cunene and Huila Provinces, which covered nearly half a million people. Namibe Province was added in 2006, but by 2008, both Namibe and Cunene were dropped and Huambo Province added. Rainfall and malaria transmission patterns in both Huambo and Huila make IRS a particularly effective intervention for malaria control for these provinces.

At the request of the NMCP in 2010, Cunene Province was once again added as a PMI IRS target province in support of Namibia's malaria pre-elimination efforts as part of the Southern

African Development Community plans for the elimination of malaria in the region. In Cunene, IRS was targeted in Kwanhama and Namakunde municipalities, including Santa Clara locality, where the population movement between Namibia and Angola is greatest. Since 2005, pyrethroids have been used in all spray campaigns, based on insecticide susceptibility testing. In addition to PMI IRS campaigns, certain municipalities in the provinces of Cabinda and Malange have, of their own initiative and funding, also implemented IRS. However, the 2011 MIS showed that IRS is available to only 7% of the Angolan population.

Progress during the last 12 months

In August 2011, PMI awarded a new contract for IRS in Angola. The partner works closely with the MOH, NMCP, and provincial and municipal health authorities. In 2012, the eighth spray round was completed in Huila, the sixth in Huambo, and the fifth in Cunene with PMI funding as part of the National Integrated Vector Control Management Strategy. A total of 136,000 structures were targeted for IRS: 60,000 in Huambo, 60,000 in Huila, and 16,000 in Cunene. The IRS spray campaign covered 98% of targeted dwellings, or a total of 145,264 structures. In real terms, this campaign protected an estimated total population of 689,668; of these 115,678 were children under five and 37,049 pregnant women. As in previous years, provincial health department staff participated actively in the 2012 IRS campaign.

To support IRS, PMI trained 1,203 people (government and private citizens) in the various components of IRS, including 609 spray operators, 414 community mobilizers and enumerators, 42 health technicians, and 14 data entry clerks.

Since significant progress in malaria control has been seen in select areas of Huambo (including the municipality of Huambo, where PMI-supported IRS efforts have focused), a plan was agreed upon with the NMCP to stop IRS in Huambo Province and move to Bie. However, upon reevaluation, the NMCP, DPS of Huambo, and PMI decided to continue spraying in Huambo Province to solidify the gains made there. Therefore, Bailundo Municipality in Huambo Province, which now has the highest burden of malaria in the province, was selected for IRS in 2013, replacing Huambo Municipality.

Entomology

Routine entomological monitoring has been challenging due to lack of an insectary, limited human resources for training, limited experience in entomology, and continuing difficulty in finding sufficient numbers of *An. gambiae s.l* to test. In 2009, an entomologic survey in Huambo Province showed relatively low numbers of *Anopheles* mosquitoes but susceptibility of 94% to lambdacyhalothrin, the insecticide being used. In October 2010, a pre-IRS insecticide resistance evaluation carried out in Huambo and Huila Provinces, using *An. coustani*, indicated 100% and 95% susceptibility to deltamethrin and bendiocarb, respectively.

The 2012 susceptibility study showed *An. coustani* collected from Huambo and Huila Provinces were 100% susceptible to deltamethrin, fenitrothion, and bendiocarb; and *An. gambiae s.l.* collected from Huambo, Huila and Cunene Provinces showed varying levels of susceptibility to deltamethrin with 94%, 94% and 98% mortality, respectively. In February 2013, insecticide resistance testing was again carried out using mosquitoes from sprayed areas in Huambo and Huila. *An. gambiae s.l.* from Huila was fully susceptible to bendiocarb but showed signs of possible emerging resistance to deltamethrin with 95% mortality. *An. coustani* from Huambo were fully susceptible to deltamethrin, fenitrothion and bendiocarb. Since there were insufficient *An. gambiae s.l.* collected in Huambo to complete the testing, several species of mosquitoes, *An. gambiae s.l, An. d'thali, An. theileri* and *An. pretoriensis*, were combined for testing against deltamethrin and bendiocarb. This mix of vectors showed 100% susceptibility to deltamethrin and bendiocarb but since *An. pretoriensis* contributed 66% and 86% of the mix for each respective insecticide, these test results are more indicative of the susceptibility of *An. pretoriensis* to these two insecticides.

For continued quality assurance of the IRS program, WHO cone bioassay tests were carried out in November 2012 to determine the quality of spraying activities and insecticide decay rates. In the absence of entomological support in Huila and Cunene, the bioassays were conducted in seven neighborhoods in Huambo on IRS-treated surfaces (deltamethrin). Adult mosquitoes reared from field-collected larvae were used since there is no access to a susceptible mosquito colony in Angola. Initial tests conducted within 10 days after insecticide application showed an average mortality of 80%, which was less than expected, probably linked to the quality of spraying. Intensive refresher training for the spray operators was conducted. Cone bioassays performed post-refresher training showed improved quality, with 98% mortality. Five months after the spraying, the mortality decreased to 52%.

Mosquito collections in Huambo Province from November 2012 through March 2013 using CDC light traps next to persons sleeping under untreated nets in IRS areas showed that of 1,297 mosquitoes, 98% were Culicines, 1% were *An. coustani,* and 1% were *An. gambiae s.l.* In the non-IRS areas, 89% of 307 mosquitoes collected were Culicines, 8% were *An. coustani,* and 3% were *An. gambiae s.l.* CDC Atlanta is supporting analysis of the mosquitoes collected for insecticide resistance testing and other entomologic monitoring activities for species identification.

In addition, PMI's implementing partner established a working insectary in the central office in Huambo Province to support entomological activities, including rearing larvae collected in the field to adulthood for insecticide susceptibility testing; conducting quality assurance of the IRS campaign; assessing insecticide decay rates; and identifying the vectors to determine species. To build capacity for entomology, PMI also trained 12 entomology technicians and provided them with opportunities to support entomological monitoring activities throughout the year. With FY 2013 funds, to better monitor PMI-supported vector management activities, the PMI implementing partner is setting up a container insectary in Huambo for continued entomologic monitoring, as the existing mini-insectary is not big enough to sustain a mosquito colony.

Proposed activities with FY 2014 funding: ($3,245,000)

PMI envisions transfer of some IRS components to the GRA and is encouraging the NMCP and DPS to share responsibility for elements such as training of IRS spray operators, M&E, and BCC for IRS. This is an important step to promote sustainability of IRS in the country; details are not yet available as discussions are still in the early stages. During the MOP FY 2014 development process, discussions were held between the PMI and NMCP teams on the future of Angola IRS. It was jointly decided to reduce PMI efforts from three provinces to one. As the NMCP is currently developing a proposal to request the GRA to support IRS in the provinces surrounding Huambo Province to ensure continued progress of malaria control in that province, the NMCP requested that PMI continue to spray in Huambo Province. PMI Angola will continue to spray in Huambo Province, but operations will expand from Bailundo Municipality to include two more municipalities in that province. PMI will cease direct support for IRS in Huila and Cunene Provinces; this will be implemented after the spray round planned for October 2013. PMI does not expect the NMCP or the province to continue IRS in these provinces; however, Huila and Cunene will both receive nets through the universal coverage campaign in 2013/14. In addition, to further ensure a responsible exit, PMI will support epidemiologic and entomologic surveillance in those areas, starting in 2013 (prior to the last spray round). As there is some geographic and activity overlap with the PMI-supported epidemic preparedness and response (EPR) activities, these activities will be integrated.

1. Support IRS in three municipalities in Huambo Province (including Bailundo Municipality); it is estimated that 100,000 structures will be sprayed. FY 2013 funds will be used in part to procure IRS-related commodities and support planning activities for the FY 2014 spray round ($2,300,000).

2. PMI will continue to support routine entomologic monitoring for both IRS and ITNs and capacity building for both the NMCP and the vector control staff at provincial level in Huambo. Entomologic indicators that will be monitored include mosquito vector species and density; insecticide resistance (annually); quality of spray operations; and residual efficacy in all provinces where PMI is supporting IRS activities. The Huambo insectary (established with FY 2013 funds) will serve as a facility for training and capacity building of the personnel in the provinces involved with entomologic monitoring of IRS and also those involved with monitoring of the national ITN program. In addition, the insectary will facilitate capacity building at the central level to assist the NMCP in their efforts to implement a central-level reference entomology laboratory ($450,000).

3. Currently there is no capability within Angola to process the mosquito materials collected during insecticide resistance testing and vector species/density monitoring. The materials will have to be sent out of country for PCR testing for mosquito species identification, insecticide resistance mechanism testing, and ELISA for determination of sporozoite rates. Using FY 2014 funds, CDC headquarters will continue to provide assistance in this area until there is capacity within Angola to conduct this analysis ($30,000).

4. In collaboration with the NMCP and DPS, PMI will continue enhanced integrated surveillance in former IRS areas (selected municipalities in Cunene and Huila and Huambo Municipality). This activity is partially starting in FY 2013 and is planned to be a rolling surveillance system. Data on outpatient cases will be collected by the implementing partner's surveillance team at one facility in each of the three levels of health facilities in each municipality for one week every month. This system will be merged with the EPR support PMI currently provides ($400,000).

5. Technical assistance visits for entomologic monitoring and resistance testing; support for specific reagents and other laboratory diagnostic materials for molecular species identification; evaluation for *kdr* genotyping and ELISA for mosquito infection rates. This amount includes cost of equipment and supplies for the aforementioned tests, materials for the insectary in Huambo Province, as well as funding for two four-week CDC tours of duty ($65,000).

Malaria in Pregnancy

Background

The NMCP's policy on malaria in pregnancy consists of a three-pronged approach made up of use of ITNs, IPTp with at least two doses of SP, and prompt and effective case management of acute malaria. The NMCP began implementation of IPTp in 2005. As of October 2012, WHO recommends that IPTp be given to all pregnant women at each scheduled ANC visit, except during the first trimester. This policy will be applied countrywide, including in areas of low malaria transmission. PMI partners are currently working with the NMCP and the Reproductive Health Department to update the manuals and training tools in accordance with the new policy and will assist with the roll-out. In the NMCP Strategic Plan 2011-2015, the target is that 100% of pregnant women who are eligible for IPTp and have access to prenatal appointments will receive IPTp with SP. Treatment of malaria in pregnancy consists of quinine for the first trimester and ACTs for the second and third trimesters. There is a sufficient stock of quinine, but there are sporadic stockouts of ACTs in different provinces.

To date, insufficient progress has been made with IPTp coverage. Data from the 2011 MIS showed that only 18% of pregnant women received two doses of IPTp and only 26% slept under an ITN the night prior to the survey. Reasons for the low rate are multiple including overall limited ANC services, weak implementation of IPTp policy, lack of appropriate policy guidelines, and lack of needed ANC staff training and supervision materials. In Angola, SP is supplied by the National Directorate of Medicines and Equipment (DNME) as part of essential medicines to health facilities. Occasional stockouts are seen at the health facility level due to lack of a proper distribution plan and poor management of drug supply to health facilities; but there has always been sufficient stock of SP in the country. Priorities of the MOH include improving availability of SP at health facilities and increasing ANC coverage, which, when coupled with systems strengthening activities, can result in more pregnant women having access to malaria prevention and treatment. The NMCP is currently working with the Reproductive Health Department on updating malaria diagnostics and treatment guidelines for pregnant women based on WHO's new recommendations.

Progress during the last 12 months

PMI continues to support NGOs and FBOs in 9 of the 18 provinces nationwide to improve access to malaria prevention and treatment services for pregnant women (eight through the NGO strengthening project and one additional province through the USAID integrated health systems strengthening project). Although many health workers have been trained to prevent, manage, and treat malaria during pregnancy, implementation of malaria in pregnancy prevention efforts is being led by the NMCP instead of the Reproductive Health Department, resulting in missed opportunities in ANC clinics. PMI continues to advocate for closer collaboration between the NMCP and the Reproductive Health Department and for sharing and better use of data for management decisions. NMCP data from 2012 showed that 38% of pregnant women attending ANC clinics in the public sector received two doses of IPTp.

Proposed activities with FY 2014 funding: ($100,000)

PMI will continue to collaborate with the NMCP and Reproductive Health Division to strengthen prevention, diagnosis, and treatment of malaria in pregnancy. The NMCP is interested in utilizing community health workers, where they exist, to reinforce community behavior regarding malaria prevention and control; this may begin with malaria in pregnancy messaging. As PMI supports NGOs that have relationships at every level in the province, this may be an avenue to pursue to improve uptake of IPTp.

1. Continue to support NGOs and FBOs in IPTp implementation and effective case management of malaria by conducting training and supervision of health workers and ensuring SP is available ($100,000).

2. Support routine LLIN distribution through ANCs (further description and costs covered under the ITN section).

3. Support BCC on malaria in pregnancy (including IPTp, LLINs and case management of malaria in pregnancy), which could include utilizing community health workers (further description and costs covered under the BCC section).

CASE MANAGEMENT

Malaria Diagnosis

Background

In 2011, Angola introduced universal diagnosis, based on WHO recommendations. Data collected through a parallel system[7] to the national health management information system (HMIS) shows that a significant proportion (69% in 2012) of malaria cases being tested by microscopy or RDT. Data from the PMI-supported NGOs shows that an average of 72% of suspected malaria cases are tested by microscopy or RDT. While there are concerns about data quality, this represents considerable progress, especially considering that the NMCP is still in the process of scaling up access to diagnostics.

PMI has invested heavily in improving access to quality diagnostics, providing microscopes and laboratory supplies. In addition, since 2007, PMI has supported the training and mentorship of 11 national level laboratory trainers and supervisors. Furthermore, it has supported training of laboratory staff in nine provinces through NGOs (reaching eight provinces through the PMI-

---

[7] This data is collected from health facilities by the municipal malaria focal points, transferred to the provincial supervisors and OPPM's which then transfer the aggregate data to the NMCP.

supported NGO strengthening project and a ninth through the USAID integrated health systems strengthening project).[8]

The NMCP continues to use multispecies SD Bioline as the RDT of choice to identify *P. falciparum* and *P. vivax*. This decision was made in 2011 based on findings from two studies that showed the previously used single-species Parachek test had lower sensitivity compared with SD Bioline. PMI, the GRA, and the Global Fund have been procuring RDTs; however, there are reports of frequent stockouts.

Progress during the last 12 months

Since 2007, PMI has procured and delivered to all provinces over 4 million RDTs and over 200 microscopes and malaria microscopy kits. The GRA is increasing its procurement of RDTs and additional supplies will be provided through the Global Fund. However, in 2015, the current Global Fund grant will end. Thus, PMI plans to provide a temporary increase in RDTs to ensure adequate access to diagnostics (based on the WHO recommendation of a ratio of two tests per every case of malaria).

In 2013, PMI, with additional support from ExxonMobil, supported a workshop to assess the proficiency of the 11 senior laboratory technicians who have been mentored by the NMCP and PMI since 2007. An additional 23 laboratory technicians from 12 provinces were also trained during this period by the joint NMCP/PMI team. These technicians will form the core training team for the country (with the former already utilized as national trainers).

In addition, PMI supports stand alone and in-service trainings on malaria microscopy and RDTs. PMI supported the standardization of training materials, job aids, and quality assurance guidelines for malaria diagnostics. In the eight provinces with PMI-supported NGOs, there are over 900 laboratory technicians, with over 300 of them trained in the last year and a half. PMI expects to have all laboratory staff trained in these provinces by the end of 2015. The integrated health systems strengthening project conducted in-service refresher trainings for laboratory technicians on malaria diagnosis by microscopy in four Luanda municipalities.

In FY 2012, the NGO strengthening project conducted 160 laboratory assessments in the eight provinces to evaluate the performance of the health facility laboratories and identify gaps which could be addressed through their support. Results showed significant gaps in multiple areas: few laboratory technicians and limited capacity; lack of functioning microscopes; insufficient supplies and reagents; lack of registration books and poor registration. In addition, they implemented quality control through slide rechecking in six of the eight provinces. The quality control exercise evaluated 1,308 slides and showed an average accuracy of 86% across the provinces (range 78% to 97%); sensitivity of 88% (range 71% to 99%); and specificity of 90% (range 81% to 94%). The project maintains a database to ensure that all relevant personnel at health facilities receive training and trainings are not repeated.

The gap analysis for RDTs below is from a quantification exercise conducted by NMCP and partners with PMI support in March 2013. Procurements for 2013 were based on a gap analysis

---

[8] Both or these projects work in Huambo province but in separate municipalities.

done for the Global Fund proposal in 2011, but the expected number of fever cases and diagnostic needs have since been revised based on a data review in a recent PMI-supported quantification workshop. The current quantification is based on HMIS data, while taking into accountunderreporting. Thus, it appears there could be a significant surplus of RDTs in 2013. PMI's stocks were delivered in December 2012 but the Global Fund supply has yet to be procured. Because the Global Fund procurements are delayed and there are reported stockouts in the health facilities, the MOH is currently in the process of procuring 2 million additional RDTs. One hundred thousand RDTs have already been purchased and the remaining 1.9 million are in the process of being procured. PMI will monitor the timing of procurements by other partners and use HMIS data to determine whether the quantification needs to be readjusted. PMI will then adjust future PMI procurements accordingly.

Gap Analysis for RDTs

	2013	2014	2015
Expected fever cases in public sector	4,868,057	5,142,523	5,431,726
Expected cases diagnosed clinically	1,217,014	771,378	0
Expected cases diagnosed by microscopy	1,460,417	1,460,417	1,086,345
Expected cases diagnosed by RDTs	2,190,625	3,059,801	4,345,381
EXPECTED PROCUREMENT			
Angolan Government	2,000,000	3,000,000	3,000,000
GF Consolidation Round (R7 Ph2 + R10 Ph1)	4,086,181		
PMI	900,000	750,000	1,300,000
Total Available	**6,986,181**	**3,750,000**	**4,300,000**
Gap	**-4,795,556**	**-690,199**	**45,381**

Proposed activities with FY 2014 funding: ($2,125,000)

PMI plans to continue to build capacity in health facility laboratories to ensure quality microscopy. PMI also plans to ensure access to and proper use of RDTs. These efforts, combined with those outlined in the Malaria Treatment section, will help ensure quality care for patients presenting with fever.

1. Procurement of laboratory supplies for microscopy kits (slides and reagents) and limited equipment for minor microscopy repairs. Distribution costs are covered under the Pharmaceutical Management section and distribution location is determined in collaboration with the NMCP. ($100,000).

2. As the Global Fund support for RDTs will end in 2013, access to testing will be critical if progress in malaria control is to continue. Thus, PMI proposes to increase RDT procurement by funding 1.3 million RDTs (multi-species SD Bioline) ($1,300,000).

3. Continue to support training, both workshops and in-service (this includes trainers, training materials, job aids), support supervision and quality assurance for parasite-based diagnosis. Additional training on basic microscopy maintenance will also be provided to extend the life of existing microscopes. This will be done in the eight provinces with PMI-supported NGOs (Zaire, Uige, Malange, Kwanza Norte, Kwanza Sul, Benguela, Huila and Huambo) ($700,000).

4. Two TDYs from CDC headquarters to support diagnostic training and quality control ($25,000).

Malaria Treatment

Background

The NMCP's 2015 target is for 80% of the population with uncomplicated malaria to have access to ACTs within 24 hours of onset of symptoms. However, the 2011 MIS shows that only 12% of children under five with fever in the two weeks preceding the survey received an ACT the same or the next day after the onset of the fever. While this is an improvement from the 1.5% seen in the 2006/7 MIS, significant efforts are needed to reach the NMCP's target.

Currently, there are three first-line ACTs: AL, AS/AQ, and DHP. The NMCP standard training manuals on treatment of malaria were updated in April 2013 to reflect these three regimens. Oral monotherapies, including chloroquine, are still widely available in both the public and private sector. Availability of monotherapies is due to multiple factors: no approved medicines list, no enforcement at the borders and ports, and multiple levels of the public system with the authority to procure health commodities (more detail in the Pharmaceutical Management section).

PMI continues to support training of health care workers in the appropriate diagnosis and management of malaria, but significant supervision is necessary to ensure adherence to malaria case management and the continued rational use of antimalarials. The policy for the treatment of severe malaria includes parenteral quinine, artemether and artesunate, with quinine still the most widely available drug. With decentralization of the government system, municipalities are free to buy the health commodities they want. This presents a great opportunity (and a significant challenge) for PMI to reinforce, at the municipality level, the importance of procuring only those treatments that are approved by the NMCP and are of known quality, approved through the WHO Prequalification Program.

As part of PMI's commitment to ensuring that all persons with malaria are promptly diagnosed and treated with a safe and efficacious antimalarial drug, PMI-financed ACTs have been procured and distributed in all 18 provinces of Angola through the public sector since 2006. PMI has historically provided the majority of the ACT needs for the country. In recent years, the GRA has increased its procurement of ACTs and the Global Fund grant will provide a significant quantity in 2013.

The GRA has built an impressive number of health facilities over the last several years and the numbers of doctors and nurses have also significantly increased. However, human resources for health are still critically low and the distribution of these resources is heavily concentrated in urban areas, despite malaria's devastating impact in the rural and hard-to-reach areas of the country. In addition, there are many foreign doctors working in the health sector with limited experience in diagnosis and treatment of tropical disease, including malaria. The integrated health systems strengthening project was designed to address some of these critical gaps that affect all aspects of healthcare.

Progress during the last 12 months

PMI supported capacity building of the health workers for diagnosis and treatment of uncomplicated and severe malaria as well as malaria in pregnancy (including IPTp) in the public sector and to a limited extent in the private sector (through a pilot program providing subsidized ACTs in the private sector). In the eight provinces supported by NGOs, there are over 13,000 health workers in the last year and a half, and over 2,500 of them have received training. This was done through formal training and in-service training. PMI has also supported the revision and production of the training manuals and job aids for malaria treatment. Training on case management is combined with training on malaria in pregnancy (including IPTp), pharmaceutical management, and record keeping.

There are four types of support supervision: provincial teams (with PMI NGOs) to municipal health department or health facilities; municipal health department teams (with PMI NGOs) to health facilities; PMI NGO technical support visits to the municipal health departments; and PMI NGO support visits to health facilities. PMI-supported NGOs aim for 90% of health facilities to receive at least one supervisory visit every quarter from the municipal health department by 2016. Over 2,000 supervisions have been carried out in the last year and a half. In collaboration with ExxonMobil, PMI has been able to train more than 1,000 nurses in malaria case management and has conducted over 1,000 support supervision visits(included in the training and supervision numbers noted above) for both health workers and laboratory technicians in these provinces in FY 2012.

The USAID health systems strengthening project has developed a tool to evaluate the standards of clinical performance on malaria, which is awaiting approval by the NMCP. They have also supported the updating of the pre-service curriculum for malaria in nursing schools in Huambo Province and have provided over 400 in-service trainings on malaria diagnosis and case management in Huambo and Luanda Provinces.

In addition, PMI procured and distributed more than 3.7 million ACT treatments in FY 2012 (part of the order was distributed in December 2012 and the remaining supplies will be delivered early June 2013). The Global Fund will procure approximately 1.5 million ACTs. The GRA procures treatment for severe malaria and has also increased its procurement of ACTs, which in combination with PMI's and the Global Fund's procurements, has been sufficient to cover the country's needs.

The gap analysis for ACTs below is based on a quantification exercise conducted by NMCP and partners with PMI support in March 2013; in addition the GRA has significantly increased its planned procurement for 2014 and 2015. As with RDTs, the procurements for 2013 were based on a gap analysis done for the Global Fund proposal in 2011, but the expected number of fever cases and diagnostic needs have since been revised based on a data review in a recent PMI-supported quantification workshop. The current quantification is based on HMIS data taking into account underreporting. Thus, it appears there could be a significant surplus of ACTs in 2013 and 2014, should all planned procurements go forward. The Global Fund supply has yet to be procured. PMI will monitor the timing of procurements by other partners and HMIS data to determine whether the quantification needs to be readjusted and will adjust future PMI procurements accordingly.

Gap Analysis for ACTs

	2013	2014	2015
Suspected Fever Cases (Public Sector)	4,868,057	5,142,523	5,431,726
Positivity Rate in the Public Sector (includes microscopy, RDT and clinical diagnosis)	55%	44%	28%
Number of Malaria Cases in the Public Sector (based on the positivity rate)	2,677,431	2,262,710	1,520,883
Prevention of Stockouts (5% buffer)	133,872	113,135	76,044
Total Need ACTs	**2,811,303**	**2,375,845**	**1,596,927**
EXPECTED PROCUREMENT			
Angolan Government (AL and AS/AQ)	400,000	900,000	900,000
GF Consolidation Round (R7 Phase2 + R10 Phase 1)	1,515,816		
PMI	3,710,000	3,000,000	700,000
Total Available	**5,625,816**	**3,900,000**	**1,600,000**
Gap	**-2,814,513**	**-1,524,155**	**-3,073**

Proposed activities with FY 2014 funding: ($5,100,000)

PMI plans to continue to support strengthening of the existing human resources for health to appropriately diagnose and manage malaria and to support preservice training to ensure the upcoming generations of health workers can properly assess and treat malaria. PMI plans to hold strategic dialogues with the NMCP and the MOH to influence malaria commodities policy and to help them develop a plan to continuously increase their procurement of ACTs and other relevant commodities. In addition, PMI plans to procure a limited supply of ACTs to complement the GRA contribution.

1. Based on the revised gap analysis above and the increased planned procurements by the GRA, PMI plans to procure 700,000 ACT treatments. PMI will work with the NMCP to prioritize locations for the distribution of these commodities ($700,000).

2. Continue to provide training and supportive supervision to health care workers in eight provinces with PMI-supported NGOs (Zaire, Uige, Malange, Kwanza Norte, Kwanza Sul, Benguela, Huila and Huambo) and limited expansion into other provinces prioritized by the NMCP. These funds would not only include the costs for training (trainers, training materials, job aids), but also BCC for prompt diagnosis and treatment of fever, capacity building of the NGOs, health systems strengthening, and pharmaceutical management outlined in the respective sections ($4,400,000).

Pharmaceutical Management

Background

A recent restructuring of the health supply chain management system in Angola closed the former central medical stores, Angomedica, and moved responsibilities for procurement, storage, and distribution of health commodities to a new parastatal organization, Central Unit for Procurement and Provision of Medicines and Medical Supplies (CECOMA). This was due in part as a response to significant thefts of PMI- and MOH-financed commodities from the central medical stores and airport in 2008 and 2009. PMI has since supported an augmented supply chain system delivering PMI-procured commodities directly to each of the 18 provincial level warehouses. The provinces then assume responsibility for the ultimate delivery to health facility level. PMI, through an integrated project supported by USAID, has been supporting the strengthening of the supply chain system for several years. However, based on findings from this partner, the central public system is not yet strong enough to reliably handle PMI-financed commodities. PMI will continue, therefore, to implement the parallel supply chain until evidence demonstrates the presence of a more robust logistics and supply chain in Angola.

Proper quantification and forecasting of malaria commodities have been challenges due to lack of consumption data, poor population estimates as there has been no census since the 1970s, and a weak logistics management information system. In late 2012, an assessment of the medicines regulatory system for Angola supported by PMI and USAID outlined several key issues affecting the supply chain:

1. There is a national pharmaceutical policy, but the law to regulate medical supplies is still in draft. Although there are legal provisions for all pharmaceutical products to be registered, registration is not occurring routinely, allowing products that are substandard or of questionable quality to enter into the public and private sectors.
2. Licensing of private pharmacies is required, but there are insufficient human resources to evaluate and provide licenses to these facilities.
3. Inspection of private sector pharmacies and pharmacovigilance are also weak.
4. The quality control system remains underdeveloped. While semiquantitative quality control measures such as Minilabs® are used at ports and border crossings, the capacity for rigorous analytical testing of drugs at the central level with a national testing laboratory does not exist. Samples of medicines are sent to Portugal or Brazil for independent testing.
5. An assessment of the supply chain system also identified key weaknesses: limited human resource capacity and lack of written guidelines and standard operating procedures.

As mandated by DNME, National Essential Drugs Program bears responsibility for procurement and distribution of malaria commodities (in addition to all other non-HIV/AIDS essential medicines and equipment). Lists of required health commodities are submitted to the National Essential Drugs Program by each of the disease programs and the requisite commodities are procured. The National Essential Drugs Program procures through local suppliers and occasionally, small donations from international donors are accepted by the GRA, some of which may include antimalarial drugs. In addition, multiple levels of the GRA administration procure health commodities, often with no guidance on ensuring procurement of quality products.

As in many other parts of sub-Saharan Africa and Southeast Asia, drug quality is also a significant concern in Angola. In late 2012, the DNME seized a large shipment of counterfeit ACTs at the port in Luanda. It alerted all public facilities and private pharmacies that an additional shipment had infiltrated the market and took measures to confiscate these products. As noted, the GRA does not yet have a qualified central level laboratory or an adequate surveillance system to systematically evaluate the quality of pharmaceutical commodities coming into Angola, but it is working on developing these systems. After this counterfeit shipment was found, PMI reprogrammed funds to support the GRA to develop a post-marketing surveillance system; activities will likely commence mid/late 2013. In addition, the USAID integrated supply chain strengthening project is working with the DNME and the General Inspector for Health to improve the regulatory functions at the central level to ensure that only quality malaria products approved by the NMCP are brought into the country for use in both the public and private sector.

Progress during the last 12 months

The process of delivering PMI-procured commodities directly to the provincial warehouses has been functioning well and is very efficient. PMI-procured supplies are usually delivered to all provincial warehouses within two weeks of arrival in the country.

In spite of this quasi-parallel system, PMI recognizes the need to engage in capacity building and the development of sustainable systems and therefore continues to support supply chain strengthening through multiple channels: the USAID integrated supply chain strengthening project; the USAID integrated health systems strengthening project that works with municipalities in Huambo and Luanda Provinces for budgeting, planning and M&E; and the NGO strengthening project in eight provinces that supports activities at the health facility level.

In late 2012, a PMI implementing partner assisted the NMCP to quantify and forecast malaria commodity needs for 2013 through 2015. In addition, they facilitated the clearance and delivery of PMI-procured commodities to the provincial level. Finally, they conducted supportive supervision in four provinces (Huambo, Huila, Cunene, and Benguela) to improve reporting on consumption. In 2012, the scope of work of this project was focused more specifically on strengthening capacity of the collection, flow, and use of commodity information, from the health facility to the national level and back. The partner is specifically working with the NGO strengthening project and integrated health systems strengthening project to develop a functional model for a logistics management information system model appropriate for the provinces in which these projects work, with the plan to scale up to all provinces nationwide.

In addition, the supply chain strengthening project routinely conducts the End User Verification Survey (a tool that assesses the availability of key malaria commodities at health facility level), most recently in 40 health facilities across 10 provinces in late 2012. The survey showed that 11 of the facilities had stockouts of various bands of ACTs and six facilities had a stockout of SP on the day of the visit. There were multiple types of ACTs stocked, creating confusion as to what to dispense, reinforcing the need for more robust supervision to better educate health-care staff on appropriate malaria case management and the rational use of antimalarials. The survey results are reviewed by the NMCP and the lower levels of administration to try to address the identified stockouts and inform the program on training needs for not only stock management, but also case management.

The NGO strengthening project also provided training of warehouse managers and pharmacy technicians, in-service training on stock management, and reporting and support supervision to provincial and municipal warehouses in the eight provinces where they are active.

Proposed activities with FY 2014 funding: ($850,000)

PMI plans to continue to strengthen the supply chain system at all levels while still continuing to use the augmented distribution mechanism for PMI-procured supplies until it can be demonstrated that the national supply chain and logistics system can securely manage and efficiently distribute large volumes of goods. PMI, through the integrated supply chain strengthening project, is working with CECOMA and the GRA on agreed-upon benchmarks to indicate when PMI can confidently transition PMI-procured products back into the national distribution system. PMI plans to continue to strengthen the regulatory and quality control system for medicines to ensure quality products are procured and minimize substandard or counterfeit drugs entering the market. PMI plans also to advocate for reducing the cumbersome clearance process for life-saving commodities.

1. Provide support for import/clearance, distribution and management of PMI-funded AL treatments in order to overcome the complex clearance process, and initial distribution from port of entry through central warehouses and down to the provincial level ($400,000).

2. Provide support for supply chain strengthening at all levels of the system. This will include support for quantification of malaria commodities; strengthening of CECOMA, including support for a logistics management information system; supporting improvements in the regulatory system through advocacy for policy approval; and enforcement and assistance with developing a monitoring strategy and tools. In addition, PMI will support for training, supervision job aids and reproduction and distribution of supply chain tools at provincial, municipal, and health facility levels, prioritizing Luanda and Huambo ($450,000).

3. Continue to strengthen the provincial and municipal pharmaceutical systems through training, support supervision, and provision of job aids and tools in the eight provinces with PMI-supported NGOs (costs included in the Malaria Treatment section).

Private Sector

Background

The private sector in Angola, which includes private clinics, pharmacies, drug shops, and street vendors, provides treatment for about 40% percent of malaria cases. Lack of availability of ACTs and poor regulation in the private sector encourage treatment of fever cases with monotherapies by untrained businesspeople, which can lead to misdiagnosis and antimalarial resistance.

In 2008, PMI assisted the NMCP to implement a pilot project in selected municipalities in Huambo Province to improve accessibility and effective use of ACTs in pharmacies through subsidized sales of Coartem. This project was launched in July 2009 and since then Coartem has been sold at private pharmacies registered by the Huambo DPS. A total of 95 licensed private pharmacies were trained by the project. Routine supervision is jointly conducted by the DPS and implementing partner staff to ensure correct implementation and adherence to national strategies and protocols.

All costs recovered were recycled back into the program to help manage overhead costs as well as to support various related projects and other ongoing activities, including the repackaging of Coartem.

Progress during the last 12 months

This pilot project is considered a major success. The pilot began in 2 of the 11 municipalities in the province and gradually expanded to all the municipalities in 2011. To date, 198 private pharmacists out of the existing 221 in the province are enrolled and trained on treatment of uncomplicated malaria. When the project began in 2012, the first two weight groups (B6 and B12) were introduced in 181 pharmacies at a subsidized price. By the end of 2012, pharmacists were trained on the other two weight groups, B18 and B24, which enables pharmacies to treat all age groups; this will be launched in June 2013. Another positive result of the project is the observed strong commitment to participate by private pharmacists and their adherence to established guidelines for dispensing ACTs. The project is strictly monitored by the DPS and project staff through routine supervision and visits by mystery shoppers. Supervision data show improvement in pharmacists' knowledge of case management of uncomplicated malaria. Preliminary data show a modest decrease in monotherapy sales with a 24% decrease in artesunate and a 16% decrease in amodiaquine. Unfortunately, pharmacists still achieve a greater profit margin in selling monotherapies.

Unlike ACTs, rolling out RDTs in private sector pharmacies has been a challenge, as it is not a national policy in Angola to allow non-clinically trained people to take blood samples, regardless of the amount. The DPS in Huambo has expressed willingness to allow pilot sale of RDTs, provided that pharmacists are appropriately trained in blood safety and appropriate use of RDT as a tool to diagnose malaria. Discussions are still ongoing and current plans are to introduce RDTs in local private pharmacies by September 2013, provided the project is able to finalize a timeframe for training. The NMCP supports the introduction of private sector RDTs and will work with DPS Huambo on expediting the process.

Recent data has shown that Huambo Province currently has the second lowest malaria prevalence in the country. Most of the recorded malaria cases are now coming from neighboring provinces, and the NMCP encourages efforts to help reduce malaria transmission in these provinces. With the Global Fund consolidated Rounds 7 and 10 grants, sales of ACT and RDTs in the private sector were to expand to include Huila and Benguela Provinces. However, insurmountable challenges led to the withdrawal of the grant's sub-recipient responsible for this component. Negotiations are still ongoing for a new subrecipient.

Proposed activities with FY 2014 funding: ($800,000)

Monitoring and implementing private sector sale of ACTs in Huambo Province are to be turned over to the NMCP and the DPS in Huambo, while the project begins implementation of private sector sale of ACTs in pharmacies in Uige Province. The PMI team plans to provide technical assistance to the NMCP and jointly supervise the project. A post-pilot survey is proposed in Huambo to evaluate its impact and feasibility of rolling out similar activities in a new province. Results of the expanded pilot will be communicated to the NMCP so that they can make a decision about rolling out this approach in other provinces.

1. Continue to build the capacity of the private sector to diagnose and treat malaria through subsidized sales of ACTs and RDTs, including training and support supervision in select areas of Luanda ($800,000).

EPIDEMIC SURVEILLANCE AND RESPONSE

Background

With the gains made in malaria control in Angola, epidemic surveillance and robust response in the face of potential outbreaks will become increasingly important. Historically, epidemic surveillance has been prioritized in the mesoendemic unstable transmission areas in the south. Specifically, in late 2008, PMI-supported the provincial health teams in southern Angola to develop plans for epidemic detection and containment, and WHO helped establish the EPR system based on collection and analysis of routine health facility data. Training and support supervision of provincial and municipal supervisors and of health facility staff for EPR has been done with Global Fund Round 7 and PMI support through WHO and the NMCP in four southern provinces (Namibe, Cunene, Huila, and Cuando Cubango).

Progress during the last 12 months

In collaboration with the NMCP, WHO continues to provide training and support supervision to strengthen capacity of health facilities, municipalities, and provinces on EPR. However, response to outbreaks has been difficult. Usually the outbreak is identified late, limiting intervention options. In 2012, this system was able to detect an upsurge in malaria cases in Namibe Province, but unfortunately was not able to detect a larger outbreak in Cuando Cubango Province. In the last year, outbreaks have occurred in areas of high transmission (Lunda Norte and Uige provinces). The GRA responded by conducting rapid refresher trainings for clinicians and distributing LLINs, RDTs, and ACT. They also set up mobile clinics and conducted BCC campaigns to alert the population. In addition, in late 2012 and early 2013, there was an outbreak in the city of Luanda, which historically has had very low transmission, but an adequate response could not be mounted.

Proposed activities with FY 2014 funding:

There is still a significant need to strengthen and even expand the EPR system in Angola. However, the malaria partners in Angola need to critically evaluate the existing system and develop a plan to ensure timely outbreak detection and response. As an EPR system has been established in most of the provinces where PMI supports IRS and can conduct enhanced surveillance, PMI will combine these activities where appropriate. Support for this activity is included in the enhanced surveillance outlined in the Indoor Residual Spraying section.

INTEGRATION WITH OTHER GHI PROGRAMS

Background

Angola has embarked on a revitalization of municipal health systems within the context of decentralizing health services. This is intended to improve infant and maternal health, as well as increase overall access to primary health care by the Angolan people. The program, led by the MOH with the support of several donors, including UNICEF, the World Bank, USAID, the Cuban Government, the Spanish Cooperation, and the GAVI Alliance, has the following components:
- Capacity development of the local public health network for the provision of an essential integrated health package;

- Fixed and outreach strategies to deliver services in health units and hard-to-reach communities; and

- Training and microplanning to strengthen integration of service delivery, including IMCI and BCC.

The revitalization process is intended to improve the quality of existing services, staff training and supervision, availability of essential medicines, diagnosis of communicable diseases, and integration of service delivery. Community outreach is planned through municipal health days to provide communities with an integrated package of health interventions including ITNs, vaccinations, deworming medications, and other essential services. The decentralization process has placed planning and coordination of the municipal health days with the provincial and municipal health authorities and the GRA allocates $2 million per municipality to support this effort each year. MOH estimates that municipal health days will reach at least 80% of the population in targeted areas.

PMI supports the NMCP in this revitalization and decentralization process, mainly through the USAID integrated health systems strengthening project and the NGO strengthening project. Both projects work with the NMCP to develop or adopt guidelines and with the municipal leadership to develop administrative, financial, and technical capacity to ensure improved access and quality of all health services including malaria.

Progress during last 12 months

In the past year, the NMCP, via its cross-sectoral technical working group, has continued to integrate its work with other health programs, such as IMCI, Well Child and Vaccinations, Nutrition, Reproductive Health, and EPI, under the framework of the Angolan health sector development plan. The NCMP has been working closely with other national implementation bodies including the National HIV/AIDS Prevention Commission, Inter-agency Committee for Immunization, Country Coordinating Mechanism for the Global Fund, various UN organizations including WHO, UNICEF, and United Nations Development Program, multi- and bilateral organizations, such as USAID, Japan International Cooperation Agency, and others.

Proposed activities with FY 2014 funding:

Building on the activities implemented in 2012 and 2013, PMI plans to continue to support NMCP's cross-sectoral technical working group to integrate work with other health programs, such as revitalization, IMCI, Well Child and Vaccinations, Nutrition, Reproductive Health, under the framework of the Angolan health sector development plan. *(Costs are included in the sections of Prevention, Case Management, Capacity Building, and M&E)*

BEHAVIOR CHANGE COMMUNICATION

Background

The purpose of Angola's 2007-2012 National Malaria Communication Strategy is to guide implementing partners and service providers. The communication strategy addresses misconceptions and seeks to improve knowledge in key behaviors essential to achieve sustained malaria control. Angola uses a three-pronged approach consisting of education, social mobilization, and BCC across the four main malaria interventions: vector control (IRS, LLINs and larviciding), case management, IPTp, and epidemic preparedness and response. The NMCP is currently working on a revised national BCC strategy for malaria covering 2013-2018.

With support from PMI and the Global Fund consolidated Rounds 7 and 10 grants, health education communication campaigns have greatly increased. Key messages on television and the radio include promotion of correct net use, importance of malaria prevention during pregnancy, and the importance of prompt diagnosis and treatment of malaria with ACTs. In 2013, BCC efforts are being intensified to ensure that messages about ownership and use of bed nets are reaching as many people as possible in order to complement NMCP's universal ITN coverage efforts. PMI supports coordination of BCC activities through the Malaria Partner's Forum.

Progress during the past 12 months

A malaria BCC campaign was launched in April 2012, with the purpose of increasing knowledge of malaria's risk factors and to change individual and community behaviors. Activities included community outreach using face-to-face discussions, drama shows on malaria, and mobile videos; training of health and community workers; radio spots; and printed messages together with those that accompany packaged ITNs and ACTs. Implementation of these activities occurs at various locations, including clinics, homes, religious institutions, schools, and community events. During FY 2012, 4,120 spots were aired on national television and 360 national radio spots were aired. Efforts were also made in 2012 to educate teachers on the prevention of malaria, with the goal of including malaria prevention messages as part of regular school curricula. PMI supported the development of training manuals for activities with children and teachers and performed theatre dramas in schools in May and June 2012. Implementing partners also gave seminars at churches and health centers to educate attendees, mostly women, on ways to prevent malaria and keep their families healthy.

The NMCP's capacity to coordinate and monitor all malaria-related BCC activities carried out by the NMCP, provincial governments, Global Fund and PMI implementing partners, and other in-country stakeholders in Angola remains a major challenge. No standardized method of estimating or counting the number of people reached through BCC activities exists, and reporting is addressed on an activity-by-activity basis.

To address these challenges, PMI is currently supporting the NMCP to revise the national malaria BCC strategy. The revised communication strategy will address malaria BCC coordination issues and provide guidance on the role that each of the malaria BCC partners should play in strengthening coordination at the national, provincial, and municipal levels. In addition, with FY 2013 funds, PMI is currently supporting the National Malaria Partners Forum to ensure effective implementation and coordination of malaria control interventions including BCC with focus at community level and on capacity building at the central level.

In terms of tracking people reached, reliable data is only available for the eight provinces supported by PMI. For example, over the last year, 33 people have been trained to relay messages to target groups; nearly 63,000 individuals in these target groups were reached through group education sessions in health facilities and communities; 34 radio programs were aired (PMI has not tracked the number of people who listen to these programs frequently as the costs for media tracking prohibitive in Angola); and over 2,500 pamphlets and posters were distributed.

With FY 2013 funds, PMI plans to evaluate BCC activities to better inform the selection of BCC approaches and messaging. The activities outlined below will reflect the outcomes from this evaluation.

Proposed activities with FY 2014 funding: ($1,300,000)

PMI plans to complement Global Fund activities and, under NMCP guidance, focus on the development of communications materials for mass media and community-based activities, interpersonal communication, preseason transmission malaria prevention activities, and case management of malaria. Evidence-based messages focused on a target audience will be used and support will be provided to the NMCP to begin to evaluate specific interventions and actual behavior change. PMI also plans to support the future development of a new National Malaria Communications Strategy in 2013.

> 1. Support for the national BCC campaign (radio spots, billboards, television spots) and development and revision of existing materials, reproduction, dissemination to target audiences, and evaluation of BCC materials for malaria communications. The BCC activities will focus on increasing ITN use by the general population, with emphasis on vulnerable groups including pregnant women and children under five; improve adherence to results of laboratory diagnosis for prescribing treatment by health care providers; and prompt, appropriate treatment with ACTs provided by public and private sector facilities. These funds will also support technical assistance for the development of the National Malaria Communications Strategy and a Monitoring Plan. The funds may also be used to support community health worker activities such as a toolkit. PMI-supported BCC activities will be closely coordinated with other partners, including the Global Fund BCC activities to maximize the best use of malaria BCC resources ($800,000).

> 2. Support BCC activities through interpersonal communication at health-facility level and community-based activities in eight provinces supported by PMI to improve adherence to treatment regimens and IPTp during pregnancy; regular LLIN use by the general population, focusing on vulnerable groups including pregnant women and children under five; improve adherence to results of laboratory diagnosis for prescribing treatment by health care providers; and prompt, appropriate treatment with ACTs ($500,000).

MONITORING AND EVALUATION

Background

Despite a weak information system and lack of any recent population figures (the last national census was done in the 1970s), several community-level surveys have been conducted, and the NMCP strongly emphasizes M&E in its program. HMIS data on malaria indicators is routinely collected through a parallel system through the municipal malaria focal points, aggregated at provincial level by the provincial malaria supervisor and provincial malaria officer, and sent to the NMCP for analysis and use for decision-making. There is a full-time M&E specialist at the NMCP supported by the Global Fund who provides significant support to the program.

However, completeness, timeliness, and accuracy of HMIS data still remain significant concerns for the NMCP and the MOH overall. Health facilities can be using multiple registers, making data tallying challenging. Because of critical shortages in staffing, there is limited time to complete the registries and weekly and monthly reports. Often these reports have to be hand carried to the municipal level, which affects timeliness and overall submission (this is one of the reasons why NMCP set up a parallel system). PMI partners provide training, supervision, data quality checks, and reporting tools to the health facilities where they work and are looking into ways to facilitate data transmission.

PMI has supported two MISs: 2006/7 and 2011. PMI plans to support another survey in 2014. The 2014 MIS will be powered to get accurate estimates at the provincial level rather than in transmission zones, as have been used previously, to assess the validity of the current zone division. The methodology and sampling time frame will be similar to the last MIS, so no issues with comparability are expected. This will also help PMI evaluate its programs as most are at provincial level. The Global Fund has agreed to co-fund this survey. Under-five mortality estimates will also be included.

PMI and the NMCP supported an impact evaluation of the scale-up of malaria activities since 2006 on all-cause mortality in children under five in 2012. The draft report is being reviewed and will be finalized before the end of 2013. The main challenge of the evaluation was the lack of data; the main evaluation was limited to the 2006/7 and 2011 MIS, and mortality estimates came from the 2011 survey only. In addition, the sampling for each survey was done at a scale much larger than that at which malaria prevention activities are implemented, making correlating morbidity and mortality from these surveys with scale-up of interventions difficult.

The table below summarizes the M&E activities that have been carried out in Angola since 2006.

Data Source	Year[5]							
	2006/7	2008/9	2010	2011	2012	2013	2014	2015
Household Surveys[1]	2006/7: MIS (report and data set available)	Integrated Survey on the Welfare of the Population (combined with Multiple Indicator Cluster Survey) (report available, data set not available)		MIS (report and data set available) – PMI supported			MIS (planned) – PMI and GF support	
		2008: Luanda epidemiolo-gical survey		LQAS on LLIN coverage in 7 provinces(repor t available) – PMI supported				
Other Surveys[2]			End User Verificatio n Survey (EUV)	LLIN durability study; EUV	LLIN durability study; EUV	EUV	EUV	EUV
Malaria Surveillance and routine system support[3]	2007: Entomolo-gic survey (Luanda, Cunene, Namibe, Huila)	2008: Sentinel surveillance at health facilities in 4 provinces	EPR system; sentinel sites stopped	EPR system	EPR system; routine entomolo-gic monitoring	EPR system; routine entomolo gic monitor-ing		
Other Data Sources[4]				Impact Evaluation				

[1] List all household surveys and the years they were conducted or are planned to be conducted. Highlight if report and/or dataset is available. Include non- or partial PMI funded surveys.
[2] List all other surveys (national and sub-national), including health facility surveys and EUV. Highlight if report and/or dataset is available. Include non- or partial PMI funded surveys.
[3] List all PMI funded surveillance and routine system support activities, including sentinel surveillance, epidemic detection and response or IRS disease monitoring.
[4] List any other relevant data sets.
[5] Years listed should reflect when PMI began in the country.

Progress during the last 12 months

PMI's support for HMIS strengthening resulted in the coordination between the National Institute of Statistics and the MOH, as well as the drafting of core indicators to be used in the National Health System (all institutions related to the health sector) to monitor progress of HMIS strengthening. Progress on HMIS strengthening will be monitored through completeness and timeliness of malaria data reported to the national levels as well as the number of facilities, municipalities, and provinces reporting. It will also be monitored through the numbers of reports generated from these data and the extent that these data are used to inform programmatic decisions. PMI has also supported the development of the NMCP M&E plan and the annual reports from the NMCP.

PMI supported the development of a training database for municipalities to track staff who have been given training, by topic, in an effort to minimize duplication and ensure that staff are provided with the requisite skill sets. In addition, a supervision database has been introduced to track supportive supervision from both the health facility and the municipalities. PMI's NGO strengthening project has also placed great emphasis on M&E for the NGOs and has conducted trainings and data quality assessments for all of the operating NGOs.

The NMCP and PMI (led by a CDC Atlanta Epidemic Intelligence Service Officer and the NGO strengthening project) have just completed a therapeutic efficacy study of two of the three first-line antimalarials for uncomplicated malaria (AL and DHP) in Zaire (mesoendemic stable transmission) and Uige (hyperendemic transmission) Provinces. Results from this study are expected in late 2013.

Proposed activities with FY 2014 funding: ($425,000)

PMI plans to continue to support strengthening of the HMIS system and routine malaria monitoring activities. PMI will also consider supporting the NMCP to develop a quarterly bulletin of province-level malaria data for use by the MOH, the provinces, and other partners.

1. Continue routine end-use verification/monitoring of the availability of key antimalarial commodities at the facility level every six months ($150,000).

2. Support the second round of monitoring the therapeutic efficacy of first-line antimalarials in the two sites established in 2013, Zaire and Uige. This will include AL, AS/AQ, and DHP ($150,000).

3. Continue to support HMIS strengthening at national, provincial, and health-facility level. This includes supporting the roll-out of the M&E plan for the NMCP including training on the indicators and the tools to track the data required to report on these indicators ($100,000 plus support included in the NGO budgets under the Case Management section).

4. Continue enhanced surveillance in former and current areas of IRS implementation (costs and further description covered in the IRS section).

5. Two TDYs to support M&E; this will primarily focus on the enhanced epidemiologic surveillance outlined in the IRS section ($25,000).

CAPACITY BUILDING AND HEALTH SYSTEMS STRENGTHENING

Background

Support to the health system is crucial for the long-term sustainability of PMI investments, and systems strengthening activities, such as training and supply chain management, have been implemented since the launch of PMI in Angola. USAID's overall approach to health systems strengthening is through the provision of technical assistance to various levels in the government in the areas of HMIS, human capacity building, and logistics and supply chain management.

USAID Angola's major project for health systems strengthening has been implemented since October 2011 and focuses primarily on strengthening human resources capacity and HMIS in the provinces of Huambo and Luanda, with funding from the President's Emergency Plan for AIDS Relief (PEPFAR), family planning, and PMI. This integrated project works closely with the MOH at the national, provincial, and municipal levels with the goal of improving capacity for service delivery, leadership, management, and supervision skills of health workers to deliver quality care and services. At the central level, the project provides support to the MOH with technical assistance in the decentralization process, whereby municipalities are responsible for a significant portion of planning, budgeting, and financial management of health resources. The program also supports the implementation of the National Health System Strategic Information Plan and works to improve effectiveness and efficiency of human resources at the municipal level. To improve service delivery, the project uses a quality improvement approach that supports standards-based clinical practices and strengthened capacity of health workers to provide family planning, HIV, and malaria services through pre-service training of trainers and nursing school teachers.

The critical lack of human resources outlined previously affects the ability of the GRA and civil society to provide essential services to the Angolan population. The NGO strengthening project supports capacity building of local NGOs with the goal that these organizations will eventually provide services for the GRA with GRA or other donor funding. This project provides training and mentoring of the involved NGOs in all areas of organization (administration, finance, logistics, operations, technical capacity, and M&E).

The Field Epidemiology and Laboratory Training Program (FELTP) is a collaboration between CDC, the *Agostino Neto* University, and the MOH. This program trains health personnel in field epidemiology. Participants acquire skills in data analysis, epidemiologic methods, and use of strategic information to make appropriate health decisions. Annually, PMI supports two students who focus on malaria for their field work.

PMI also provides funding to WHO for activities that complement those done by the USAID health systems strengthening project in the area of HMIS. The USAID supply chain strengthening project collaborates with the DNME to improve integrated supply chain management, and periodically produces end-user verification surveys to monitor stockout of essential medicines.

Progress during the last 12 months

PMI-funded projects supported municipalities in eight provinces (Zaire, Uige, Malange, Kwanza Norte, Kwanza Sul, Benguela, Huila, and Huambo) to develop health plans and budgets. Towards the end of 2012, the methodology used by municipal teams to develop plans and budgets was further reviewed, refined, and standardized. This year, these standardized planning and budgeting templates will be rolled out to all municipalities by the MOH. PMI partners also continue to develop a cadre of national, provincial, and municipal supervisors to conduct support supervision at health facilities. Support provided by partners includes supervision planning and tool development, health facility malaria report verification, and municipal and provincial level malaria reports and database management.

In addition, PMI projects promoted active review and discussion of monthly reports with municipal and provincial supervisors to foster analysis for problem identification and explore possible solutions. The focus has been on improving documentation in patient record books so that the quality of the data available for analysis improves.

PMI has also provided support to revamp the Malaria Partners' Forum. In July 2012, new executive members were elected and their first meeting was held in early 2013. The Malaria Partners' Forum assists the NMCP in coordinating all malaria partners and stakeholders in the country and is currently compiling information from all partners to develop a comprehensive inventory of all malaria activities. In addition, for the first time, the executive members developed an annual work plan and budget, which was presented to members to review.

PMI supported the NMCP in quantifying ACTs and RDTs this year through a workshop with NMCP, CECOMA, the Pharmacy Division, and the logistics members of the Global Fund Program Management Unit. The processes and procedures for quantifying medical commodities were reviewed and then consensus was reached on the data to use for malaria commodity quantification. This quantification has been used to guide FY 2014 planning.

The FELTP program has been very active in malaria activities this past year. The entire FELTP student body (ten students) participated in the investigation and response to upsurges of malaria in Lunda Norte and Cuando Cubango Provinces, and a smaller group supported an investigation of a malaria upsurge in Uige Province. In addition, one FELTP student played a critical role in the supervision of the therapeutic efficacy study of first-line antimalarials in Uige Province, and two students are in the process of analyzing the malaria surveillance systems in Bengo and Huambo Provinces.

As part of capacity building of the NMCP, the PMI Resident Advisors are embedded at the NMCP to provide technical assistance and support all coordination and implementation of malaria activities in the country. These advisors spend about 50% of their time working with NMCP staff and participating in technical meetings providing inputs on NMCP's protocol and guidelines on malaria case management. To support this year's universal coverage campaign, PMI advisors took the lead in working with an external consultant (recruited to assist NMCP with all logistics) to review the campaign macroplan and coordinate technical committee meetings.

Proposed activities with FY 2014 funding: ($800,000)

The MOH recently outlined its National Health Development Plan 2012-2015, which includes a new approach to capacity building. All clinical school curricula will be reviewed and updated to reflect current norms and policies. Health workers who are currently employed (i.e. already graduated and in the workforce) will be trained by participating in the school modules appropriate for their work and profession. PMI plans to support an NMCP pilot of the malaria component of this initiative. PMI plans to continue to support the other capacity building efforts outlined under each intervention section as well as the activities below.

1. Support human resources capacity building by embedding training of health staff for malaria case management, laboratory diagnosis, logistics management, and support supervision within existing schools of nursing and medicine in Luanda and Huambo. This will include developing pre-service curricula, establishing a strategy so that the current health workforce can be trained in the appropriate modules for malaria, piloting the implementation in Luanda and Huambo, and building the capacity of the DPS in these two provinces to plan and budget for these continued trainings and overall healthcare. It is expected that this activity will be a one-year activity, and the MOH will be able to scale it up using its own funds ($300,000).

2. Continue to strengthen provincial-level supportive supervision by the NMCP for malaria activities including technical assistance on effective supervision tools and timely and supportive follow-up ($300,000).

3. Continue to support two students from the FELTP program to focus on malaria activities; this support could also include outbreak investigation ($150,000).

4. Support the Malaria Partner's Forum to assist the NMCP and provinces to coordinate malaria partners. This includes development of a partner database with geographic coverage and scope of activities; quarterly meetings; compilation and collation of partner quarterly reports; website development to ensure resources are used efficiently, minimize duplication, and facilitate sharing of best practices ($50,000).

5. Continue to support strengthening of local NGOs in select provinces (Zaire, Uige, Malange, Kwanza Norte, Kwanza Sul, Benguela, Huila, and Huambo) (costs covered under the Case Management section).

PUBLIC PRIVATE PARTNERSHIPS

Background

Since the launch of PMI in Angola, ExxonMobil has worked in partnership with the USG and has provided $4.5 million USD to date to support case management and human capacity building efforts through PMI partner NGOs who work in eight provinces, namely Benguela, Huambo, Kwanza Sul, Kwanza Norte, Uige, Huila, Malange, and Zaire. These NGOs work closely with DPSs and coordinate all malaria control activities with local authorities.

Progress during the last 12 months

Under this public–private partnership with ExxonMobil, more than 1,000 health workers have been trained. The partnership with ExxonMobil has also supported training manuals and tools, standard operating procedures, and the training of a cadre of laboratory trainers who, with additional funding, will take to scale training and capacity building of laboratory technicians across the 18 provinces (see Diagnosis section for further details). This partnership is valued by all key stakeholders. A recent press ceremony commemorating the partnership was held at the U.S. Embassy in April 2013, with participation from the Minister of Health, the Managing Director of ExxonMobil, and the U.S. Ambassador.

Given the influx of private companies that work in Angola's oil and mining industries, the potential for private partnerships that leverage PMI funding is great. Recognizing this, the USAID Mission has decided to develop a more robust plan for building public-private partnerships to harness private funding and capacity of the private sector needed to further development goals. Toward that end, the mission facilitated the training of two staff members in October and November 2012 and will be drafting a mission strategy for securing and managing public-private partnerships in 2013. PMI will be a strategic player in the mission's public-private partnership strategy, as PMI accounts for more than 50% of the health funding in the health mission.

Proposed activities with FY 2014 funding:
The activities funded by private partners, including ExxonMobil, will continue to be implemented in close coordination with the NMCP and will take into account the results of a recent PMI-funded evaluation of the NGOs. ExxonMobil recently donated $500,000 in 2013 and provided $1 million in 2012. Private funding may also allow PMI to expand its support of NGOs to an additional province, thereby increasing the number of health care providers trained in malaria diagnosis and treatment.

In addition, PMI advisors plan to be actively involved in supporting the implementation of the mission's strategy for public-private partnerships, specifically in identifying ways that PMI funding and activities can be leveraged in scope and scale by private funding.

STAFFING AND ADMINISTRATION

Two health professionals serve as Resident Advisors to oversee the PMI Angola program, one representing CDC and one representing USAID. All PMI staff members are part of a single inter-agency team led by the USAID Mission Director or his/her designee in country. The PMI team shares responsibility for development and implementation of PMI strategies and work plans, coordination with national authorities, managing collaborating agencies and supervising day-to-day activities. Candidates for resident advisor positions (whether initial hires or replacements) will be evaluated and/or interviewed jointly by USAID and CDC, and both agencies will be involved in hiring decisions, with the final decision made by the individual agency.

The PMI professional staff work together to oversee all technical and administrative aspects of the PMI, including finalizing details of the project design, implementing malaria prevention and treatment activities, monitoring and evaluation of outcomes and impact, reporting of results, and providing guidance to PMI partners.

The PMI lead in country is the USAID Mission Director. The two PMI resident advisors, one from USAID and one from CDC, report to the USAID Supervisory General Development Officer for day-to-day leadership, and work together as a part of a single interagency team. The technical expertise housed in Atlanta and Washington guides PMI programmatic efforts and thus overall technical guidance for both RAs falls to the PMI staff in Atlanta and Washington. Since CDC resident advisors are CDC employees (CDC USDD—38), responsibility for completing official performance reviews lies with the CDC Country Director who is expected to rely upon input from PMI staff across the two agencies that work closely day in and day out with the CDC RA and thus best positioned to comment on the RA's performance.

The two PMI resident advisors are based within the USAID health office and are expected to spend approximately half their time sitting with and providing technical assistance to the national malaria control programs and partners. PMI Angola plans to hire a Program Management Specialist for malaria in FY 2013.

Locally-hired staff to support PMI activities either in Ministries or in USAID will be approved by the USAID Mission Director. Because of the need to adhere to specific country policies and USAID accounting regulations, any transfer of PMI funds directly to Ministries or host governments will need to be approved by the USAID Mission Director and Controller, in addition to the PMI Coordinator.

Proposed activities with FY 2014 funding: ($2,395,000)

PMI will continue to support staffing and administrative costs for both USAID and CDC.

1. Staffing and administrative costs for the USAID and CDC resident advisors, one full-time program management specialist for malaria, headquarter backstops, and in-country support staff and associated administrative costs ($2,395,000).

Table 1
President's Malaria Initiative – *Angola*
(FY 2014) Budget Breakdown by Partner

Partner	Geographical Area	Activity	Activity Budget ($)	Project Subtotal ($)
DELIVER Task Order 7	Nationwide	Purchase and distribution of LLINs	7,975,000	10,475,000
		Procurement of laboratory supplies for microscopy	100,000	
		Procurement of RDTs	1,300,000	
		Procurement of Coartem	700,000	
		Technical assistance and support for import, clearance, storage, distribution and management of RDT and ACT commodities	400,000	
MSH (SIAPS)	Nationwide	Strengthen Ministry of Health antimalarial drug management system	450,000	600,000
		Survey of availability of malaria commodities at the health facility level (End-use verification)	150,000	
PSI	Huambo and Uige	Subsidized ACT sales in select areas in Huambo and Uige	800,000	1,600,000
	Nationwide	National BCC campaign to promote net use and care and repair	800,000	
IRS TBD	Huambo	Indoor residual spraying	2,300,000	2,750,000
	Nationwide	Capacity building for entomologic monitoring, vector mapping	450,000	
World Learning (Eye Kutoloka)	8 provinces	Transport of LLINs from provincial warehouse to health facilities	1,885,000	7,885,000
	8 provinces	BCC to promote net use and care and repair in 8 provinces	500,000	

	TBD	Strengthen malaria case management	4,400,000	
	Nationwide	Strengthen malaria in pregnancy services at health facilities in 8 provinces	100,000	
		Provincial level supervision with NMCP	300,000	
		Technical assistance on quality control of laboratory diagnosis (microscopy and RDTs)	700,000	
Jhpiego (SASH/ Forca Saúde)	Luanda and Huambo	Facilitate malaria program implementation and health systems strengthening in collaboration with NMCP	300,000	**300,000**
CDC	Nationwide	Entomological marker testing (mosquito and LLIN processing using PCR) in Atlanta	30,000	**295,000**
	Nationwide	Entomologic monitoring and insecticide resistance testing	65,000	
	Nationwide	Technical support for laboratory training	25,000	
	Nationwide	Technical support for M&E	25,000	
	Nationwide	FELTP	150,000	
WHO	Nationwide	Strengthening HMIS	100,000	**100,000**
TBD	Nationwide	Enhanced integrated surveillance/EPR in southern epidemic prone and former IRS areas	400,000	**400,000**
TBD	Nationwide	Therapeutic efficacy study	150,000	**150,000**
TBD	Nationwide	Support to Malaria Partners' Forum secretariat	50,000	**50,000**
Total			**$24,605,000**	

$27,000,000

*Does not include budget for staffing/administration of $2,395,000.

Table 2
President's Malaria Initiative - *Angola*
Planned Obligations for FY 2014

PREVENTIVE ACTIVITIES

Insecticide Treated Nets

Proposed Activity	Mechanism	Budget		Geographical area	Description
		Total $	Commodity $		
Procurement of LLINs	DELIVER Task Order 7	7,975,000	7,250,000	8 provinces	Purchase approximately 1.45 million nets with distribution to provincial level. Provinces will include those were PMI-supported NGOs are active
Transport of LLINs from provincial warehouse to health facilities	World Learning	1,885,000		8 provinces	Transport of LLINs through ANC for pregnant women and EPI for children under five years of age using NGOs, where they are present - includes monitoring of distribution to end users
SUBTOTAL - ITNs		**9,860,000**	**7,250,000**		
Indoor Residual Spraying					

Activity	Implementer			Location	Description
Indoor residual spraying	TBD (Central Task Order to be competed)	2,300,000	165,000	Selected municipalities in Huambo	IRS in select municipalities in Huambo Province (estimate covering 100,000 households)
Assist the GRA to increase entomological capacity for routine monitoring, susceptibility studies, etc.	TBD	450,000		Nationwide with focus on Huambo	Routine entomologic monitoring (including in former IRS areas), susceptibility studies, vector mapping. Capacity building for central and provincial staff.
Entomological marker testing (mosquito and LLIN processing using PCR) in Atlanta	CDC	30,000		Nationwide	PCR processing of mosquitoes and LLINs from Angola until the capacity in Angola is sufficient to transition to be processed locally
Enhanced integrated surveillance/EPR in southern epidemic prone and former IRS areas	TBD	400,000		Huambo, Huila, Cunene, Cuando Cubango and Namibe	Development, training and implementation of a surveillance system in former IRS areas; this will be built on and merged with the EPR activities that has already been developed
Technical assistance for entomologic monitoring and insecticide resistance testing	CDC	65,000		Nationwide	Technical assistance visits for entomologic monitoring and resistance testing in

Activity	Partner	Cost	Cost	Coverage	Description
					NMCP; support for specific reagents and other laboratory diagnostic materials
SUBTOTAL - IRS		165,000	3,245,000		
Malaria in Pregnancy					
IEC/BCC for malaria in pregnancy in NGO supported provinces	World Learning	Costs covered under IEC/BCC for net distribution		8 provinces	IEC/BCC for IPTp and care seeking for malaria in pregnancy in 8 provinces. This could include using community health workers for messaging
Strengthen malaria in pregnancy services at health facilities in 8 provinces	World Learning	100,000		8 provinces	In eight provinces, improve health facility workers' understanding and compliance in administering IPTp, diagnosing and treating malaria in pregnancy, LLIN use in pregnant women and provision of tools to accurately track MIP services
SUBTOTAL - MIP		100,000	0		
SUBTOTAL PREVENTIVE		13,205,000	7,415,000		
Case Management					

55

Diagnosis

Procurement of laboratory supplies for microscopy	DELIVER Task Order 7	100,000	100,000	Nationwide	Procurement of laboratory diagnostic reagents and supplies and limited supplies for basic microscope repairs
Procurement of RDTs	DELIVER Task Order 7	1,300,000	1,300,000	Nationwide	Procurement of 1,300,000 RDTs (SD Bioline)
Technical assistance on quality control of laboratory diagnosis (microscopy and RDTs)	World Learning	700,000		Nationwide	Diagnostic quality control - this will include training on microscope basic use and maintenance
Technical support for laboratory training	CDC	25,000		Nationwide	Two TDY visits to provide assistance to in-country partners in the correct use of laboratory diagnostic test results
SUBTOTAL - Diagnosis		**2,125,000**	**1,400,000**		
Treatment & Pharmaceutical Management					
Procurement of artemether-lumefantrine	DELIVER Task Order 7	700,000	700,000	Nationwide	Purchase of approximately 700,000 treatments of artemether-lumefantrine

Strengthen malaria case management	World Learning	4,400,000		TBD	Training, support supervision for provincial and health facility health workers to improve malaria case management
Technical assistance and support for import, clearance, storage, distribution and management of RDT and ACT commodities	DELIVER Task Order 7	400,000		Nationwide	Provide assistance in the distribution from port, and storage through customs, and down through provincial level
Strengthen Ministry of Health antimalarial drug management system	Management Sciences for Health	450,000		Nationwide	Strengthen pharmaceutical mgmt. related to antimalarial drugs including regular supervision, provincial training of pharmacist, help with printing of SCM forms
Build the capacity of the private sector to manage malaria	Population Services International	800,000		Huambo and Uige	Strengthen malaria case management in the private sector in select areas of Uige and Huambo Provinces and creating opportunities for the private sector to promote quality diagnosis and treatment, data collection

SUBTOTAL - Treatment & Pharmaceutical Management		700,000		6,750,000
SUBTOTAL CASE MANAGEMENT		2,100,000		8,875,000
Behavior Change Communication				
National BCC campaign to promote ITN use as well as prompt and appropriate diagnosis and treatment	Population Services International	800,000	Nationwide	Support for the national BCC campaign and development and revision of existing materials, reproduction, dissemination to target audiences, and evaluation of BCC materials for malaria communications
BCC activities at health-facility level and community-based activities in eight provinces	World Learning	500,000	8 provinces	BCC to improve adherence to treatment regimens and IPTp during pregnancy; regular ITN use; improve adherence to results of laboratory diagnosis; and prompt, appropriate treatment with ACTs
SUBTOTAL IEC/BCC		1,300,000		
Capacity Building and Coordination				

Activity	Partner	Budget	Geographic Area	Notes
Facilitate malaria program implementation and health systems strengthening in collaboration with NMCP	JHPEIGO	300,000	Luanda and Huambo	Contribute to malaria program implementation as part of larger health systems strengthening initiative within MoH.
Provincial level supervision with NMCP	World Learning	300,000	Nationwide	Strengthen provincial-level supervision by the NMCP for malaria activities. Provide technical assistance to NMCP to visit each province at least twice a year.
Field Epidemiology and Laboratory Training Program	CDC	150,000	Nationwide	Support two students in the field epidemiology and laboratory training program to focus on malaria
Support to Malaria Partners' Forum secretariat	TBD	50,000	Nationwide	Continued support to National Malaria Partners' Forum
SUBTOTAL Capacity Building		**800,000**	**0**	
Monitoring and Evaluation				
Survey of availability of malaria commodities at the health facility level (End-use verification)	Management Sciences for Health	150,000	Nationwide	At least biannual monitoring of commodity availability and use at health facility level

Activity	Agency	Location			Description
Therapeutic efficacy study	TBD	Zaire and Uige	150,000		Evaluating the efficacy of first line (AL, AS/AQ, DHP in two sites)
Strengthening HMIS	WHO	Nationwide	100,000		Support to strengthening HMIS
Technical support for strengthening M&E	CDC	Nationwide	25,000		Two TDY visits to provide assistance to in-country partners for M&E
SUBTOTAL M & E			**425,000**	**0**	
In-country Staffing and Administration					
Staffing and administration	USAID and CDC IAA admin	Nationwide	2,395,000		Support to salaries and benefits of Resident Advisors and support staff (CDC IAA $1,160,000 and $1,235,000 for USAID)
SUBTOTAL - In-Country Staffing			**2,395,000**	**0**	
GRAND TOTAL			**27,000,000**	**9,515,000**